THE
USEFUL IDIOT

Also by S.V. Dáte

Non-Fiction

Jeb: America's Next Bush

Quiet Passion: A Biography of Senator Bob Graham

Fiction

Black Sunshine

Deep Water

Smokeout

Speed Week

Final Orbit

THE

USEFUL IDIOT

**How Donald Trump Killed the Republican Party
with Racism and the Rest of Us with Coronavirus**

S.V. Dáte

SOUNION BOOKS

ISBN: 979-8-6757-5453-3

For America

Table of Contents

Preface

I did not want to write this book. Unlike novels, where you can make sure the bad guy has an unfortunate run-in with a hungry tiger shark or annoyed badger at the end, you have no such editorial control over real life. Bad things happen, and there's nothing you can do other than write about them. It is way too much like the day job.

It's one thing if the focus of your book is an admirable person deserving of respect. That was the case with both of my previous biographies. Even though I did not personally agree with all of their decisions or views, I admired their intellect and work ethic and passion for what they believed in.

Not to give too much away, but that was not the case in this particular instance.

I've been a journalist for 35 years, working for news outlets as big as the Associated Press and NPR and as small as the Middletown, New York, *Times Herald-Record*. I've covered city commissioners and police, NASA astronauts and FEMA bureaucrats, governors and mayors, prosecutors and actual, literal murderers and thieves. In all that time, I've never dealt with anything as ridiculous yet also as terrifying as this man and this White House.

A quick note here: I came upon Donald Trump as a blank slate. I had no opinion of him at all before I first met him at a Florida Republican fundraiser in 2006. The conclusions I have reached in recent years are based on his words, his actions and my research into his decades-long background in the public eye. This is what I have concluded:

Donald Trump is the most ignorant, least emotionally stable, most openly corrupt and most cheerfully dishonest president most likely in the history of the republic, but certainly in the past century. His business career was filled with incompetence and low-rent fraud – for decades.

For three years, these traits and behaviors were inflicted on our country from the highest office in the land – yet still seemed like mere abstractions for so many Americans. A killer pandemic has changed that.

As the count of dead Americans approaches 200,000, what was apparent to those paying close attention since June 2015 is becoming more obvious to everyone: There has never been a worse fit between man and moment in our history.

And that is a story that deserves telling.

1. The Useful Idiot

A pandemic never occurred to them. The idea that Donald Trump would ever be required to sit still, pay attention and make rational decisions that would determine whether hundreds of thousands of Americans would live or die not once crossed the minds of those who put him into the Oval Office.

Oh, they all had their various reasons for wanting him there. For white evangelical Christians, he had explicitly promised to appoint the federal judges they had so longed for to turn back the nation's cultural clock. For Mitch McConnell, a Trump win – as unlikely as it seemed – was the only real path to making sure Republicans retained control of the Senate and he himself remained majority leader. And for Vladimir Putin, having Trump in the White House – as unlikely as it seemed – would be a dream come true, an opportunity to wreak havoc on his longtime adversary and weaken its historic alliance with Western Europe.

Russia's dictator, of course, was not remotely interested in what Trump's ascension might mean for Americans in the event of an actual calamity. If they were dumb enough to vote for him, well, they deserved whatever they got. In any event, it was not his problem.

As for his American supporters, perhaps so much time had passed since September 11, 2001, that the idea of a genuine national emergency was but a faded memory. Perhaps the quiet competence that Barack Obama's team had employed with the 2009 flu pandemic and later with the 2014 West Africa Ebola outbreak had diminished the perceived threat that a simple virus could present.

For whatever reason, even as they watched the noise and chaos and nonsense generated by *candidate* Donald Trump for a full year and a half, the consequences of a real crisis requiring real leadership actually happening on the watch of a *President* Donald Trump never really dawned on them.

True, there existed then – and continues to exist today – a significant cadre of Republican voters who genuinely believed that the Trump they watched on *The Apprentice* was the real Donald Trump. That he was a real billionaire, based on his own efforts and smarts. That he was capable of making rational, quality decisions based on the facts presented to him.

That excuse, though, does not work for those Republicans from Mitch McConnell on down to the congressional candidates who had occasion to speak with him in person. As one top Republican National Committee member told me after his first face-to-face encounter with Trump two months before the 2016 election: "Okay. Our guy is insane."

His was not a minority view, by the way. Trump's incoherence, his temper, his impulsiveness, his breathtaking ignorance – all of it was well known among the top tiers of the Republican machinery. But for them, it was simply a challenge to overcome, another hurdle that fate had placed between them and their holy grail of judges and tax cuts and regulatory rollbacks. Not once did I ever hear any concern that *just maybe* they were working to install a useful idiot who truly was an idiot, with absolutely zero leadership qualities one ordinarily looks for in someone aspiring to become the chief executive of the world's remaining superpower.

It was an abject failure of the Republican Party's responsibility to the country. In our two-party system, both have a duty to weed out candidates who fail the threshold test of commander-in-chief and, relatedly, emergency-manager-in-chief. Through the summer and fall of 2015 and then the early nominating contests of 2016, it was clear as day that Donald Trump was not credible in those roles, and yet neither the remaining candidates nor the party leadership made a serious effort to ensure his defeat. True, there were some who voiced warnings. Jeb Bush called Trump a "chaos candidate" who would bring us a "chaos presidency." But there was also Ted Cruz, who literally praised Trump for the better part of a year, refusing to criticize him in the hopes of one day inheriting his voters. By the time Cruz did unload on him, it was seen as sour grapes. Such was the cynicism and game-playing that put us where we are.

Republicans will pay a price for that negligence. This already became apparent in the off-year elections, with Democrats winning back the House in 2018 and scoring wins in such unlikely races as a special election for an Alabama Senate seat in 2017 and the Kentucky governorship in 2019. Whether Republicans suffer a complete presidential year wipeout in the autumn of 2020 or four years later is debatable, but that it will happen is not. Trump is betting not just his own future, but that of the party he hijacked on the dwindling demographic of angry, white men without college degrees, disproportionately in the South. This is not a winning bet.

Separate from the Republican Party's failure to safeguard the country, though, is the failure of ordinary Americans. Donald Trump did not elect himself. And while he had the direct help of Russia and the unintended help of the FBI director, it was in the end actual Americans who cast their ballots for him.

In a representative democracy, the buck ultimately stops with the voters. So, yes, the president failed us miserably in his handling of the pandemic. From pretending he had stopped the virus from entering the country to claiming it wasn't so bad to wishing that it would just go away to nonsensically hyping an unproven treatment to discouraging the use of masks to, eventually, just getting bored with it and moving on, the president could not have handled this more poorly had he been actively trying to fail us. This is on him – the many hundreds of thousands, even millions, of serious illnesses that might not have happened with a competent response. The one hundred and fifty thousand deaths, at least, that could have been avoided. But it's also on us.

When the coronavirus reckoning is complete, when all the numbers are eventually tallied, here's one more that should be included: the 62,984,828 who enabled it to happen back on November 8, 2016.

~ ~ ~

In truth, no one should have been surprised by Trump's ruinous handling of a real disaster when it arrived in January 2020. Trump himself had given us all a clear warning just a few months earlier, when he ginned up a fake one for no good reason at all.

In late summer 2019, Donald Trump wreaked chaos and confusion upon Americans trying to plan for the possible arrival of a massive hurricane along the southeast coast. As residents of Florida, Georgia and the Carolinas anxiously tracked Dorian's projected path, Trump tossed out his own forecast on Twitter, adding a new state into the mix:

"In addition to Florida - South Carolina, North Carolina, Georgia, and Alabama, will most likely be hit (much) harder than anticipated. Looking like one of the largest hurricanes ever. Already category 5. BE CAREFUL! GOD BLESS EVERYONE!"

Almost immediately, the phones lit up at the National Weather Service office in Birmingham as panicked residents called to ask if it was true. That Dorian was going to cross Florida and hit *them*. This led to a tweet from the meteorologists in that office – who at the time did not know where the misinformation was coming from – stating that Alabama was not, repeat, *not* in Dorian's path and everyone should calm down.

And that, in turn, spawned a weeks-long imbroglio with the White House and Trump's various apologists on one side insisting that Trump had been right and Alabama *had* been in danger at the time Trump posted his tweet versus the

4

meteorologists and tropical storm experts at the National Hurricane Center who pointed out that the consensus forecast was already calling for the storm to parallel the East Coast and then head off to sea. Front and center was a week-old tracking map onto which Trump had with a black Sharpie drawn in a semicircle to include Alabama.

The defenses of him afterward were largely along the lines of, well, that's just Trump being Trump. Which was both true and – although this went underappreciated at the time – downright horrifying.

It was an open rejection of expertise in a life-and-death field. What Trump was saying was that his opinion of where the storm would head and whose lives were in imminent danger was every bit as valid, because he was the president of the United States, as that of those who had devoted their adult lives to the study of Atlantic cyclones. It was beyond parody. Most stunning of all was the view within his senior staff that it was no big deal. One aide even kept on his desk a printout of the tracking chart in question, kind of as a souvenir from what he considered a ridiculous kerfuffle in which Trump had, yet again, *owned* the press.

That right there should have been a bright red flashing warning sign. Because a hurricane is a slow-moving menace that is observable through publicly available images from weather satellites and other data. What's more, the National Hurricane Center and the National Weather Service continued to do their jobs, notwithstanding the president's meddling. What Trump did was inexcusably dangerous, but only those fool enough to still be listening to the man given the track record of his first two and a half years in office were going to be negatively affected. Everyone else would listen to the Hurricane Center and local emergency management officials and act accordingly.

No, the bigger risk that became obvious with the hurricane map stunt was the possibility of a threat that truly required a competent presidential response. Trump could not even properly manage the approach of a hurricane – something that typically happens several times every single year – and then tried to coerce his executive branch agencies into revising history in an attempt to back up his silly tweet. How would he manage a threat that a president, and only the president, was in a position to deal with?

I actually mentioned that exact possibility in a long piece about Trump's endless dishonesty, and even posited the threat of a deadly disease. That article published on January 15, 2020.

Unfortunately, it was only a week later that America started to get the answer to that question.

~ ~ ~

It's easy now as the pandemic drags on and the American death toll climbs toward 200,000 to put all the blame on Donald Trump. He did, after all, make bad decision after bad decision in the crucial early weeks of the outbreak, from ignoring intelligence community warnings to downplaying the threat to avoiding taking steps that would anger China's dictator and endanger the all-important trade agreement he believed he needed in order to win a second term. He even called concerns about the pandemic "a hoax" at one of his campaign rallies, sending a signal to his voting base that public health officials have had an impossible time countering ever since.

That mishandling of the disease in turn wrecked the strong economy that for three years Trump had been claiming as his own. In truth, he had inherited it from Barack Obama, with employment and gross domestic product numbers largely similar to those under his predecessor's second term. The resulting crisis is rivaling the Great Depression in job losses. With a competent response to the pandemic, much of the related economic catastrophe might have been avoided, as well.

And yet, again, Donald Trump did not anoint himself president. That was the work of those 63 million Americans who walked into their polling places and decided to put a cartoonishly unserious person into the most serious job in the country.

6

As the pages to come will detail, there were a number of factors that led to this. Vladimir Putin decided that the best way to weaken America in 2016 was by hurting former Secretary of State Hillary Clinton in the Democratic primaries, and boosting a "reality" game show host in the Republican contests. How could he know that the 162-year-old party, which once prided itself on its hard-headed realism, would fail to do all in its power to stop him. FBI Director James Comey, for what he thought was the good of his institution, decided in late October to re-open an investigation into Clinton's misuse of a private email server. How was he to know that state polling was off, and that Clinton's expected easy win was a chimera, and that his two letters to Congress would put the election on a knife's edge.

In retrospect, it seems quaint, adorable, almost, how much time and energy and hand-wringing went into investigating Clinton's emails – given the loud and proud corruption Trump has carried out these past three years, from the funneling of millions of both campaign as well as taxpayer dollars into his own cash registers, the installation of his own daughter and son-in-law into White House positions, the use of his office and his attorney general to squash investigations into himself and his companies, the attempted extortion of a foreign leader into hurting the political rival he feared most, the begging of a dictator for a favorable trade deal to help him win re-election, the open use of his office and White House staff to stage *de facto* campaign rallies, and on and on and on and on.

The thing is, that he would behave this way was not surprising in the least. He had lived his entire adult life in this manner, and the evidence was right out in the open, from his business dealings with the mob to the way he treated his "charity" as a personal slush fund, using it for everything from buying a $12,000 football helmet autographed by Tim Tebow to paying his son's seven dollar Boy Scout dues. Sixty-three million Americans knew this, or actively chose not to know this, and decided they were fine with it.

One such voter, in fact, worked with Trump for years and knew full well about his dishonesty and treachery. He told me he didn't care. That the system needed shaking up, and that he wanted Trump to go in and be a bull in a china shop and smash things.

That person is now a senior official in the administration.

~ ~ ~

Trump's handling of the pandemic, also, was entirely predictable.

For starters, he only occasionally takes intelligence briefings. Both George W. Bush and Barack Obama began their days with one. Trump spends the first several hours of his day watching television and tweeting about what he has just seen. In 2020, he has been taking between just one and two briefings each week.

Meaning that when the experts were trying to tell him that something bad was happening in China, and that we needed to prepare, Trump could not be bothered to listen. His top health officials were getting alarming news over the New Year's holiday about a pneumonia-like outbreak in Wuhan. Trump was golfing. When his Health and Human Services secretary finally got him on the phone nearly three weeks later to talk about the virus, Trump yelled at him instead about a backlash to vaping regulations that was going to hurt Trump with vapers.

Indeed, Trump's singular focus was then, and remains today, his own re-election. Nothing else matters, and that is now why well over a hundred thousand more Americans have died than would have had just about any other adult human being been president instead of Trump.

In January, winning a second term meant getting his "trade deal" with China signed. Not a harsh word could be spoken about the country or its dictator. Never mind that it wasn't really a free trade agreement, just a partial unwinding of the trade war he had started. For Trump, it was everything. He repeatedly praised China and Xi Jinping for their "transparency" about the virus, when the opposite was true.

In February, trade deal signed, Trump saw increasing concerns about the virus as a direct assault on his re-election bid. He refused to take the pandemic seriously, even as it ravaged Italy and Iran. When a top CDC official warned that people's lives were about to change dramatically, Trump was enraged because of the stock market sell off it triggered. He told Americans via Twitter that thousands die from the flu every year and encouraged them to buy stocks. From the White House briefing room, he claimed he had done a fantastic job and that the 15 diagnosed cases to date would soon drop to zero. At one of his rallies, he even claimed that the virus had become his critics' latest "hoax," and lumped it into the category that included his acceptance of Russian help to win the 2016 election (which was, by the way, true; he had, in fact, done that) and his impeachment over his extortion of Ukraine for help to win the 2020 election (which was also true; he actually did that as well).

After seeming to take the threat seriously for a couple of weeks in the second half of March, Trump quickly grew bored of it and began demanding that states "re-open" their economies so he could go back to the campaign strategy that he had been planning, that is, taking credit for the economy Obama had left him.

Numerous times, Trump repeated in remarks what he tweeted on March 22, in all capitals: "WE CANNOT LET THE CURE BE WORSE THAN THE PROBLEM ITSELF."

Indeed, just reading back through his various statements through the course of the pandemic is an exercise in shock and awe. "The coronavirus is very much under control in the USA." "This is a flu. This is like a flu." "I think that we're doing a great job." "It's going to disappear. One day, it's like a miracle, it will disappear." "Just stay calm. It will go away." "Slow the testing down, please."

And, of course, the statement that could easily wind up the epitaph of his presidency: "I don't take responsibility at all."

If evil scientists had conspired to concoct a worse president for our country in a time of crisis, they would have been hard-pressed to outdo Donald Trump. His ignorance, mendacity and stubbornness are a toxic mix in the best of times. Many of the adults in both parties assumed that eventually, when it was finally over, his most egregious messes in the area of trade policy, the NATO alliance, climate change and the environment could, with some work, be cleaned up.

The same cannot be said for all the Americans who will have died unnecessarily because one of the worst human beings in public life – a man who has shown time and time again that his lack of humanity is matched only by his open corruption – happened to become our president.

~ ~ ~

Perhaps something good can come of this, in the end. Maybe this hard lesson will bring back the idea that the presidency is not a game. That the judgement and the maturity and the smarts of the person behind that desk matter – and not in the way that most people think.

There is a segment of the population who insist a president be "relatable," to be someone they'd want to have a beer with. Others demand that a candidate match up completely with their preferred vision of the future, of the policies they want to see enacted, and failing such a person's presence on the ballot, they will not vote at all. Still others – disproportionately younger voters – believe they have a fundamental right to demand that a candidate *inspire* them, and failing such inspiration, they also will not bother voting.

Maybe, perhaps, the election of a shameless, cheerfully corrupt con man whose selfishness and ignorance led to the sickness and death of so many of their fellow Americans will help these people grow the hell up.

We don't choose a heart surgeon or a tax accountant or an airline pilot using those criteria, and their jobs are not nearly as critical for the common good as the president of the United States. Sure, it would be nice for a president to be interesting and down-to-earth enough to seem relatable – but that's not nearly as important as competence. There's nothing wrong with supporting a candidate who shares your ideas and ideals. But making big changes takes time, and, in a crisis, an ideologue can be the worst personality to have in charge. You need someone willing to understand the world as it is, not insist on seeing the world as they feel it ought to be.

As for inspiration – we do not pick the surgeon who is funnier or the accountant who spins out the most engaging anecdotes. Why do we conflate those traits with leadership?

This is not new, by the way. People did not vote for John F. Kennedy because they believed he would bring thoughtful wisdom to the Oval Office. Ronald Reagan's people learned from that and made his entire campaign, indeed, much of his presidency, a movie production. George H.W. Bush had, hands down, the most relevant experience of any president, and had governed with a low-key self-assuredness. Clinton beat him by seeming more empathetic.

In all three of those cases, though, the winning candidates exhibited their interest in a serious approach to the job during their campaigns, and all three wound up demonstrating that in office. In contrast, Trump during his campaign showed he had little knowledge of how the world worked, and made it clear he had no interest in learning. His view was that it was all easy, and that any idiot could do it. Well, clearly, he was wrong.

Forget all the insane promises he made that were not possibly deliverable. The only real promise that the biggest slice of his base wanted was to make America like it was in the 1950s, which even they knew was not possible. They didn't care. They liked that he was willing to promise it to them, and that he was willing to smash things and make "the establishment" mad.

It is true that Trump did not even receive a plurality of the votes cast, and almost certainly would not have won without the combination of both Russian help and the Comey letters re-opening and then re-closing his Clinton investigation in the campaign's final days. Yet the fact remains that 46 percent of Americans casting ballots that day did so for someone who was not remotely qualified for the job. This, nearly four years later, remains astounding.

A significant percentage of those, obviously, were perhaps not the most informed or sophisticated of voters and believed Trump really was the savvy and smart businessman he played on television. But what about the rest? They could see what he was all about, but voted for him anyway? What does that say about their view of the importance of the job?

Maybe the coronavirus pandemic can impart the lesson that first and foremost, the person elected to the Oval Office has to be capable of handling the really bad things, the things you did not or even could not anticipate. Airlines don't pay pilots two hundred thousand dollars a year to set planes down on clear sunny days with little wind. They get paid well for their years of experience, for all the training they've had, and the training they continue to undergo, for the day that the hydraulics fail and then they lose an engine to a bird strike on final approach during a thunderstorm, with a bad crosswind. On a related note, nobody asks as they climb aboard whether the pilot is someone they'd like to have a beer with later, or what her views are on Medicare for all.

Leadership matters, as has now been made abundantly clear.

~ ~ ~

There was a terrific skit done by "Saturday Night Live" in the late 1980s, that portrayed Ronald Reagan as a doddering, increasingly detached granddad smiling and mouthing meaningless clichés to the news cameras as they demanded answers about the Iran-Contra scandal … and then, behind closed doors, transforming into a cunning mastermind who had personally directed every detail.

This, roughly, was how Trump's defenders in the Republican Party portrayed him during the 2016 election, after they were stuck with him as their nominee. It was all an act, they promised. The unhinged rants, the constant tweeting, the outlandish lies – it was all performance art, they claimed, to appeal to a segment of the population that has long been disaffected by traditional Republican politics. Behind closed doors, they promised, he was a different person. A thoughtful and reasonable grownup who sought divergent viewpoints before making decisions. This would be revealed in the off chance that he somehow won the election, particularly as the weight of the office burdened his shoulders.

These claims, obviously, were lies – or, in the case of those who did not really know Trump very well, wishful thinking.

There is no doubt that Trump can, on occasion, behave like a grownup. But as insider account after insider account confirms the evidence of our own eyes and ears, it is this occasional grownup behavior that is the act, the performance art.

The real Trump is the one who bellows angrily at his critics and opponents, the one who posts absurd conspiracy theories on Twitter, who manically calls his safe circle of fawning sycophants for advice, who openly admires authoritarians around the world while attacking and insulting democratically elected leaders, who refuses to take responsibility for any of his failings and who is willing to do anything – from extorting a foreign country to begging China's dictator to egging on open racists to delegitimizing our own coming election – to hold onto power.

The burdens of office have not weighed down on him a single bit. Compare photos of Bill Clinton, either of the Bushes or Obama before they took office and four years in. Note the graying hair, the worry wrinkles and weariness. Now look at Trump before and today. More bloat, perhaps, but a face otherwise unchanged.

He is now, and for decades has been, a middle school bully with the impulse control of a toddler. The only thing Donald J. Trump cared about before he took office was Donald J. Trump. That has not changed in these three and a half years.

~ ~ ~

What's remarkably missing in my multi-year exploration of Trump's universe is a full-throated, or frankly, even half-hearted defense of any sort of basic, human decency. People defend his "economic" nationalism. They shrug and point out the judges he has appointed and the regulations he has rolled back. Others point to the tax cut, and how he has helped their personal bank accounts. One White House aide told me that no other Republican elected in 2016 would have produced as many conservative policies as Trump has. Not one bothers to sell the idea that he is misunderstood and is at heart a good human being. Not one.

This view is not restricted to those who work with him. Over the past four years, I have done countless interviews with Republican supporters who after rattling off judges and tax cuts and deregulation nevertheless concede, in the end, that they wish he would keep his mouth shut more and tweet less or even not at all. Which is about as open an admission of what they think of him as a person as is possible. His off-the-cuff remarks and his tweets – *not* the prepared speeches people write for him to read – are the most honest reflection of his true self. When his supporters say they wish he would hide that truth, it is because they understand precisely what kind of human being he is and how that is perceived by normal people with basic standards of conduct.

Amazingly, that so often gets glossed over in all the talk about him. Sixty-three million Americans, and the quirks of the Electoral College, put into the most powerful office in the world a truly despicable person. Donald Trump does not treat people well. He would cheat you as soon as look at you. He is spiteful and mean while also venal and ignorant. And *none* of this was hidden from view. Not a single bit of it. Yet people voted for him anyway.

That says a lot about us. None of it good.

~ ~ ~

Democracy is not easy.

If there's one lesson that needs to be learned from the Trump years, it is that one. Democracy is not easy, because for many, many people on this planet and in this country, freedom is not easy. For folks who more or less have it together, that may be hard to understand.

While those who live and work in the world of ideas have the time and the inclination to ponder grand concepts and endless possibilities, a great many of our brothers and sisters struggle just to get through each day. As in literally wonder how they will manage to make it until bedtime. Whether it's anxiety or depression or the drugs and the alcohol with which they are often intertwined, so, so many people just want someone to tell them what to do and to take care of them.

It's no wonder that religions with strict rules on how to live one's life hold such appeal and are growing so rapidly. The more rules, the better.

This is the key to "populists," who understand that a substantial number of people are perfectly fine with a strong leader who promises order in a universe that appears not to have any. In his 2016 run, former Pennsylvania Senator Rick Santorum understood this even as most in his party did not. The vast majority of people are not entrepreneurs who dream of starting their own businesses. Most people just want a steady job that will be there next year and in five years and in 20 years so they can buy a house and raise children and do all the things they're supposed to do the way their parents did.

Small wonder that a craven demagogue like Donald Trump could take advantage of those insecurities and tell those people exactly what they wanted to hear.

This has always been the inherent danger in the American experiment: Self-governance requires active engagement by the citizenry. Because things rarely work out as planned, the drafters of the Constitution came up with federalism and checks and balances. On top of all that, this country has been blessed by its massive size and its attendant bureaucracy. It's hard to institute large-scale change of any kind, in any direction. People demanding action on the climate can attest to this. People pushing for universal health care can attest to this – indeed, have been attesting to this, for decades.

Despite this, the fact remains that breaking things is easier than fixing them, as Donald Trump has repeatedly demonstrated. With a 30-percent plurality of the populace interested in maintaining its cultural supremacy solidly behind him and a large enough slice of the Republican establishment willing to accept a Faustian bargain for the sake of its own agenda, he has gotten away with it.

We can already see what this has done to our country after three and a half years. What happens if that three and half becomes eight?

2. The Rogue Wave

Nobody thought he would win. Nobody. Not the Republican National Committee. Not Hillary Clinton's campaign. Not Trump's top campaign staff, many of whom were working the phones the afternoon of Election Day to start rebuilding bridges and lining up job prospects. And certainly not Trump himself, who reserved a smallish ballroom at the Hilton Midtown four blocks from his penthouse apartment where he could come in, give a perfunctory concession speech to a crowd of a few hundred, and then go the hell home.

On the camera riser there was already a hint of the next act: a small sign reserving a spot for "TRUMP TV," a network of his very own, to give him the adulation he had come to crave from the many dozens of campaign rallies he had staged over the previous year and a half.

Sure, there were the 20-something volunteers, the guys in ill-fitting suits and red "Make America Great Again" hats, the young women in slinky dresses and too-high heels. But most of us in the room were there out of personal or professional obligation. Friend or family of a campaign staffer or, like me or my colleagues, reporters who had started out covering Jeb Bush or Chris Christie or Marco Rubio and wound up following around an absurdist caricature of a presidential nominee and in just a few more hours it would all be over and we could get back to normal, rational lives. Those of us who would be covering the White House again after the election were more than a little annoyed that we were stuck at Trump's event, rather than at Democratic nominee Hillary Clinton's victory party at the

Javits Center. It was bad enough we'd wasted months hanging around with third-tier Republican campaign staff – the only sort who would take jobs with Trump – instead of the Clinton team, who would actually be running the West Wing.

At that moment, of course, nothing could be done about that, at least until Trump conceded and then we could try to race across town to the Clinton party.

All of that, though, was before polls closed in most of Florida, where I had spent some two decades as a reporter. Pasco County, north of Tampa, always reported quickly and in recent elections had become a reliable barometer for the state as a whole. Barack Obama had lost it by 7,687 votes in 2008, when he won the state by three points, and had lost it by 14,164 votes in 2012, when he won the state by just one point. My sense was that if Clinton lost Pasco by about 15,000 or so votes, she would be on track to win Florida, and if she won Florida, that was pretty much the ballgame.

But Clinton did not lose Pasco County by 15,000 or so votes. Instead, she got crushed – 52,000 votes fewer than Trump. I texted a smart political operative friend of mine from my Florida days and learned that Clinton had, in fact, hit her target turnout number in Pasco. It was just that the other side had turned out even more.

I understood that Pasco's result by itself didn't necessarily mean Trump had won Florida. I also knew that Clinton could afford to lose the state and still have a great number of paths to the White House. At the same time, I guessed that what had happened in Tampa's northern exurbs was probably not unique to Florida – that if huge numbers of white, working-class, infrequent voters had turned out there, they were probably also turning out in other parts of the country.

When North Carolina, another state the Clinton campaign believed she would narrowly win, was called for Trump, I realized my working assumptions over the previous nine months had crumbled. I had not particularly enjoyed covering Trump's campaign. He had openly courted racists to win the nomination. He had no problem spewing lies about big things and small. More than any politician I had ever covered in three decades of journalism, he was shockingly ignorant about matters central to the job he was seeking, yet was simultaneously certain of his own genius. He was, worst of all, vindictive, petty and mean.

So many Americans tune into political campaigns even as high-profile as the presidential race only in the final few weeks, and have a fairly limited understanding of the candidates and their backgrounds. True, Trump – thanks in large part to ratings-hungry cable news – was somewhat of an exception to that. Yet his outsized public profile did not necessarily inure to his benefit. He was more disliked than liked on Election Day.

And still ... I felt like most voters didn't know the half of it. So many, many of them I had spoken to on the campaign trail accepted as a given that Trump's business experience was his best asset. Even among Democrats who didn't like him for other reasons, many had bought into the notion of his managerial competence. Smart, highly educated professionals who had backed Clinton would, in the weeks before the inauguration, tell me that the country was fine. He was a billionaire businessman, after all – he couldn't be stupid.

They had no idea.

~ ~ ~

The phrase "rogue wave" conjures up an image among land-bound folks of a giant, cresting wall of water, racing across the ocean, smashing whatever unlucky vessel might be in its path.

But that's not what it is at all. In reality, a rogue wave is a function of multiple wave patterns intersecting at a particular place at a particular moment. Two or three ordinary wave trains meeting in mid-ocean so that the crests happen to coincide, creating for that instant a towering monster – or a yawning chasm. Either of which can be disastrous for the unfortunate sailor who happens upon that moment of intersection.

In November of 2016, America was that unfortunate sailor, swamped and capsized by a handful of wave patterns that happened to coincide that particular election day.

The biggest and most obvious was the bitterness of the Republican base – that thirty or forty percent of GOP and GOP-leaning voters who are still upset about the passage of the 1964 Civil Rights Act, let alone the fact of Barack Obama's two decisive presidential wins. A second major wave train was the smoldering resentment about how the recovery from the Great Recession had arrived for the well-to-do, but not for the average worker or homeowner. The willingness of evangelical Christians to set aside their erstwhile interest in a "moral" candidate in exchange for the guarantee of loading up the federal bench with like-minded judges was a third. Then there was the lesser but still significant wave generated by FBI Director James Comey's passive-aggressive investigation of Hillary Clinton's use of a private email server, which ended with a pair of seismic letters in the final days of the campaign. And finally there was Vladimir Putin's sustained efforts to hurt Clinton and boost Trump.

Given Clinton's organizational and financial advantages, Trump almost certainly would not have won had any one of those factors been absent. The constructive interference, as it's called in physics, from just four of those wave trains would not have created a tall enough crest or deep enough trough to have handed Trump the presidency. Trump and his team, naturally, claim that their victory was due entirely to their brilliant campaign strategy of focusing on the Upper Midwest states that had previously voted for the Democratic nominee in multiple elections – the so-called "Blue Wall" that included Pennsylvania, Michigan and Wisconsin. Had Hillary paid attention to those states, she would have won. But she did not, goes the Trump mythology, because she was a terrible candidate running a bad campaign.

Even accepting that argument as true – and, in fairness, she was not a great candidate – the fact remains that Trump only won by 44,292 votes in Pennsylvania, 10,704 in Michigan and

20

22,748 in Wisconsin. Less than a percentage point in each state. Trump won Florida by just over one percentage point. With margins that thin, how was the daily drumbeat of WikiLeaks and how they "proved" Clinton was "corrupt," as Trump was claiming in all of his campaign events during the final month, *not* determinative in the election? How was all the social media propaganda that appears to have successfully depressed the African-American vote nationally as well as in those key states not a deciding factor? Both of those were part and parcel Russia.

Same thing with Comey. The effect of those letters with less than two weeks to go in the campaign was to revive the endless focus on "her emails" that had largely faded and to bring it right back to the forefront. Voters who had not made up their minds, not liking either alternative, broke heavily toward Trump in the final days. Had Comey not written those letters, is there any doubt that Clinton would not have won those three states, and perhaps a couple more?

Did Comey know *his* "wave" was going to be the one that made the already building monster break? Almost certainly not. In fact, had he known how close the election was going to be, he might have held off on that October 28 letter, given his knowledge of the counterintelligence investigation into Trump. Did Putin know his efforts would put his favored candidate in the White House? Again, almost certainly not.

Not that it mattered for the country. In the end, we sailed off into Election Day expecting more or less the continuation of the previous dozen years – and instead found ourselves in the one bad spot where these massive waves happened to converge in a colossal breaker that came crashing down on our decks.

Nearly four years later, we're still clearing the debris.

~ ~ ~

The first time I saw Donald Trump in person was at a 2006 fundraiser for Charlie Crist, who was then Florida's Republican attorney general and on his way to succeeding Jeb Bush in the Governor's Mansion. The event was at Mar-a-Lago, the Palm

Beach resort Trump had bought eleven years earlier, and I arrived a few minutes late and well into a detailed explanation from Trump about the ceiling molding in that particular room, the flooring, the chandeliers, how much he had spent, how classy it all was, and by the way, had we seen his television show, "The Apprentice," on NBC? It was the number-one rated show on television now for a couple of years, maybe the best-rated show of all time, even, and ….

On and on he went, for what seemed like an hour. Usually at these functions, the host introduces the candidate, who then goes on to give a modified version of his stump speech and then, to make the donors feel like they're getting something for their money, might take a few questions. That did not happen that summer evening. Trump, in fact, barely even acknowledged Crist, who was left to stand beside him the whole time, nodding in agreement as Trump talked about how great he and his businesses and his television show were.

Afterward I came to understand that this was simply how Trump was. He was not a major player in Florida politics or a big donor. His only real interest in statewide legislation was a perennial – and perennially failing – effort to bring casino gambling to Florida. But the state Republican Party humored him. What was the harm, after all?

Nine years later, the harm finally became evident. Allowing Trump's clearly false boasts about his tremendous wealth and unrivaled business acumen to go unchecked for a full decade and a half on prime time television created the monster that swallowed the entire Republican Party, put American democracy in an existential crisis, and inflicted the coronavirus on our nation to an extent unimaginable by other wealthy countries.

It's true the United States has had inept and venal presidents before, although those adjectives are, in some measure, in the eye of the beholder. But what's clearly true is that in the post-war years, we have never put into the White House someone with less knowledge about the country and the world, with no interest in acquiring any, and with absolutely zero compunction about using the presidency to profit himself and his children.

~ ~ ~

Looking back, the great irony of that evening was that several of us Florida statehouse reporters a year later thought that one person in that room might well have a shot at the presidency someday. We just totally misread who that was.

Crist wound up running as smooth a campaign as we'd ever seen, making sure to lock up Jeb Bush's supporters while also playing to moderate Democrats and, especially, the Black community. In a Democratic wave year, Crist won the governorship comfortably. A little over a year later, after he had delivered a narrow win to Arizona Senator John McCain in the Florida presidential primary, it seemed like Crist had a real chance at the running mate slot and, with that, a road to altering the trajectory of the Republican Party. Crist was pro-consumer, good on the environment, at the cutting edge on climate change, pro-immigration, and had a strong relationship with the state's African Americans and Latinos.

How wrong we were.

McCain did not in the end choose Crist, and the subsequent election of Barack Obama in 2008 set in motion the events that proved both the downfall of Crist as well as the rise of Trump. Obama traveled to Florida to promote his stimulus package to help the economy amid the worst downturn since the Great Depression. Crist not only supported the legislation, but he physically embraced the first African-American president on stage in Sarasota. That hug ended up being his undoing in his run for Senate the following year.

Trump, meanwhile, noticed the parade of openly racist hate against Obama forming up in the "Tea Party" and associated conservative groups and quickly raced to the front of it by becoming the most prominent backer of the conspiracy theory that Obama wasn't really born in the United States and was therefore an illegitimate president.

Indeed, the "birther" movement and its attacks on Obama are probably the best lens for examining what happened in 2016.

First, it is a testament to this country's progress that it is no longer acceptable to say "I don't like Barack Obama because he is Black." It sounds ridiculous, but it was not all that long ago when hearing that kind of talk was fairly common in many parts of this country.

So it was that starting from the time it became clear in 2007 that Obama had a serious chance of winning the Democratic nomination, one of the most common phrases pollsters and journalists began hearing in voter interviews became: "I'm not a racist, but…"

It is remarkable how many responses I personally have received after asking about Obama that have started out *I'm-not-a-racist-but* ... but then, over the course of the interview, it would become pretty clear that yes, the 44th president's skin color appeared to have a great deal to do with the interviewee's views on the matter.

A backlash to the first Black president, in fact, goes a long way toward explaining the coalition that came together to put the antithesis of Obama into the Oval Office.

Donald Trump is, hands down, the least knowledgeable, the least curious, the least prepared, the least-capable-of-ever-*being*-prepared president to be sworn into office in at least the last century.

Even his biggest claimed asset, his "TEN BILLION DOLLAR" net worth (Yes, he really did put it in all capital letters in a news release) earned as a "self-made" businessman is total fiction. He took the equivalent of a billion dollar inheritance and managed, after four decades, to have barely gained anything – a remarkable accomplishment, given the growth in the economy over that time period. Back in the late summer of 2015, I calculated for a *National Journal* story that had Trump taken the $200 million he was worth in 1982 a few years after assuming control of his father's company and just invested that money in the stock market, he would have been worth some $8 billion by the time of his presidential campaign.

24

That number is nearly three times the $2.9 billion that Bloomberg News estimated he was worth in 2015 (even that estimate was deemed high by those who have spent the most time studying his family business).

Transforming the reality of "bad" or "mediocre" businessman into the myth of "super genius international tycoon" took a number of years and itself required a confluence of various factors, which will be explored in greater detail in the next chapter.

The important point is that the facts about Trump were available for the Republican Party primary voting base. A plurality chose not to seek out those facts or to believe them when confronted with them. Some of that can be attributed to Americans' predisposition to admiring rich people, particularly those who started from humble roots (as Trump falsely claimed he had). The rags-to-riches storyline has been a favorite in this country for many generations – so many people see that possibility for themselves, someday.

But in the summer and autumn of 2015, Trump's creation myth was not what was driving his popularity. Rather, it was his eagerness to show that of all the dozen and a half Republican candidates running, he was hands down the one who hated Barack Hussein Obama the most. He was the one who railed against "political correctness," which, in many of his supporters' minds, meant not being able to call the president the N-word. He was the one who was going to shut down the border and throw out all the "illegals" and end the travesty of granting citizenship to their children who are born here.

They wanted someone who talked and acted just like them, in other words. And, absent any adult leadership from the Republican Party or any sustained pushback from the other candidates, they got him as their nominee.

And once that had happened, most of the contributing factors to that rogue wave that eventually put Trump into office were fully in place.

~ ~ ~

Of course, it did not take long after Trump had moved into the White House that the purported reasons his supporters had cited most often to back his candidacy dried up and blew away. He did not bring an efficient managerial style to the West Wing, which became a chaotic, nonsensical place on day one and remains so today. He did not bring any great "deal-making" skills, either, as evidenced by the trade war with China and the rebranded but essentially unchanged trade agreements announced with much fanfare with South Korea and Mexico and Canada.

Indeed, the sole "talent" Trump seems to have brought with him to the White House was the ability to invent his own reality, regardless of the facts, and then relentlessly sell it to the public, day in and day out – presumably with the idea that such a small slice of the population is actually paying close attention that he is more likely than not to eventually persuade a large percentage of voters that he is actually telling the truth.

In New York that had meant saying his buildings were the tallest and the most luxurious and his women were the most beautiful. In the White House, having already attained a position that only 43 others had achieved over the span of two centuries, the go-to boast was obvious. He was not just a great president, but the best president who had ever lived.

Astonishingly, he began this almost immediately upon taking office, claiming that no president had ever gotten off to as fast a start as he had. By May, it was that no previous president had gotten as much done in the first 100 days. And by the time of the 2018 midterms, Trump was claiming that his presidency, regardless of what was still to come, already belonged in the history books because of all his accomplishments – to the point where he even started talking about getting himself carved onto Mt. Rushmore.

At an Oval Office photo opportunity in early 2019, Trump spoke as if of course everyone knew how great he had done, and that was why Democrats were working so hard to block money for his border wall.

26

"Now they say it's the wall, because I've accomplished practically everything else. Look, I accomplished the military," Trump said. "I accomplished the tax cuts. I accomplished the regulation cuts. I accomplished so much. The economy is the number-one economy in the world. We're the number-one economy in the world. We're the number one, not even close. Companies are pouring into our country. I've accomplished so much. So now they say, 'Oh, if he doesn't get the wall' – they make that the only issue. But it's not going to work, because I'm building the wall. The wall is happening right now, okay?"

Over and over and over, day after day, week after week, Trump would claim that he was overseeing the best economy in American history (he wasn't). That his tax cuts were the biggest ever (they weren't). That his increases to military spending were so huge as to be historic (Other presidents, including Obama, had larger ones).

Bizarrely, Trump did not just contain his lies to things that needed some level of expertise or time spent in research. Often he would try to deny things for which the facts were blindingly obvious. On that same January day he strung together all the false boasts about his accomplishments, at a later event Trump claimed that his intelligence chiefs had not, in fact, reported that Iran was actually in compliance with the nuclear deal, that ISIS had not really been defeated and that North Korea was not interested in getting rid of its nukes – all in direct contradiction to Trump's boasts.

Trump confirmed to reporters that he had called CIA Director Gina Haspel and Director of National Intelligence Dan Coats to complain. "I did. And they said that they were totally misquoted and they were totally – it was taken out of context. So what I'd do is I'd suggest that you call them. They said it was fake news, so – which, frankly, didn't surprise me."

Of course, Haspel and Coats had been testifying in open hearings on Capitol Hill. Every word of what they said had been broadcast live. There had been no misquoting, no "taking out of context."

This is just one example. There are hundreds of others. Thousands. If there is any unifying theme of the Trump presidency, in fact, it is its singular dishonesty. Trump will lie about anything and everything, issues large and small, from morning until night. I asked one former top White House aide why Trump did that, and he just started laughing. "He lies like he breathes."

As he tried to bully congressional Democrats to spend billions of American tax dollars on a border wall that he promised hundreds of times he would make Mexico pay for, Trump began inventing tales about why a wall was necessary. El Paso, Texas, he said, was living proof. Before a wall was built, crime was rampant. After it was completed, it was the safest city in the United States. Need more reasons to build a wall? How about all the women who were kidnapped and tortured and bound and gagged with blue duct tape and thrown into the back seats and trunks of cars and smuggled across the border in the remote desert where there was no fencing?

Naturally, not a word of that was true. El Paso was one of the safest cities of its size before a border fence was built, and it remained so after it was completed. As to the bound and gagged and duct-taped women – that was a peculiar bit of misogynistic fantasy that Trump genuinely appeared to enjoy telling. It was unclear where he got it, although some theorized that he had either seen or heard about a crime movie that depicted something similar.

~ ~ ~

Absolutely zero of this behavior, of course, should have come as a surprise to anyone who had spent even a half hour becoming familiar with the Donald J. Trump of the 1980s, 1990s, 2000s and the first half of the 2010s. This is who he is, and this is who he has been for decades.

In fact, that's what much of the Republican establishment was saying about him when he started running in 2015 against what had been considered an all-star roster. At that first debate that August, when Trump insulted the others, the audience in the arena booed him. Over the coming months, early front runner Jeb Bush called Trump the "chaos candidate" and warned that he would be a "chaos president." Others called him a pathological liar and a con man.

But then, as Trump began looking certain to win the nomination, wholesale amnesia took hold within the Republican Party, from RNC leaders to state party operatives to big-dollar donors, right down the line. They realized the direction of the new wind and adjusted their attitudes and views accordingly. The temper tantrums and childish taunts they had only recently ridiculed, they instead started explaining away as strategic, performative theater.

It was, they insisted, an act. It was all for show, because what was Donald Trump, really, but a master showman? Underneath the facade he put on for the cameras, he was thoughtful and deliberative and rational. We would see, they told us.

Over and over, I was given these reassurances. That it was all fine. There was nothing to worry about. The country would be in good hands, in the miniscule chance that hell froze over and pigs sprouted wings and Donald Trump somehow was elected president. One longtime RNC member and donor who had been a key member of previous Republican presidential campaigns told me that with Chris Christie in charge of staffing the executive branch, a hypothetical Trump White House would have competent people doing the real work, even if Trump himself wound up behaving as nutty in the Oval Office as he had on the campaign trail.

And, indeed, there were some grains of possible truth to the tales these folks were spreading. When Trump was asked at the end of his second debate with Clinton what positive thing he could say about his opponent, he came out and declared that he admired how she fought for what she believed and never gave up. On election night, his victory speech was almost gracious. And during the transition, in his meeting with the *New York Times* editorial board, Trump was downright reasonable. He even started out calling the *Times* the "jewel of American journalism" and gave reasonably rational responses to the many questions. (This extended interview, by the way, was far more supportive of the notion of a "normal" Donald Trump than the prepared speeches that sometimes dazzled gullible cable television commentators. Those were written by others, and all Trump had to do was read them aloud. The *Times* visit was totally unscripted.)

Of course, after every such case of seeming normalcy, in a matter of days or sometimes just a few hours, Trump would go right back into the churlish, over-the-top nonsense that we seem to see far more often.

If his defenders are correct, then he is "in character" – playing the boorish, politically incorrect "alpha" male – most of the time. Which of course leads to the possibility that the exact opposite of what his apologists are selling is true: Trump is in reality exactly who he appears to be. An old man with the emotional state of an immature 11-year-old boy, born to wealth, with strong opinions but very few facts to back them up and an irrational certainty in his own abilities. And it is the calm, rational, "normal" Trump that is the act, the character he slips into when he absolutely must.

From a practical standpoint, of course, it doesn't matter whether there is a hidden, normal Trump if that personality never has functional control. It may matter to the research psychiatrists in years to come, but it does not – and should not – matter to everyday Americans.

For us, the real Trump is the one we see each day. The childish taunts (that he evidently thinks are brilliant), the belligerent tone, the constant and pointless chaos. That is who he is, that is who he has been through his entire adult life, and that is what Americans should expect for his remaining days in the White House, however many that might be.

~ ~ ~

Evangelical Christians found their holy grail in the flood of federal judges they believe will bring back 1950s America. The corporate donor class got their rubber stamp for a drastically lower tax rate that certainly put a lot more money back into their pockets. But the biggest winner of all was the guy who legally wasn't even supposed to have a say in any of this.

Indeed, if there was any person happier than Breitbart publisher Stephen Bannon as Donald Trump descended his escalator to join the Republican presidential field that June day, it was Vladimir Putin, the former KGB spy and now perennial "president" of Russia, some 4,700 miles away in the Kremlin.

Why this fact was not more alarming to the voting public in the summer and autumn of 2016 perhaps speaks to the general ignorance of Americans to things beyond our nation's borders. Maybe people assumed, with the Cold War over, who the Russian leader is and what he wants really doesn't matter to us anymore. Maybe they believed Russia's leader today is still in the vein of Boris Yeltsin, a big, slightly drunken teddy bear, incapable and uninterested in causing us any harm.

Putin, of course, is an entirely different animal. He trained as a KGB intelligence agent and was deployed to East Germany in the years that the secret police there routinely did torture and murder, often in consultation with Moscow. Putin entered politics after his spy days, only to see the empire he had served crumble around him. And unlike forward-looking, would-be reformers like Yeltsin, Putin saw Russia's best days in the past, as the iron fist in the steel glove of the Soviet Union.

So when the promised reforms didn't pan out and life did not get better, or did not get better quickly enough, Putin was right there, offering hope and strength in the past. With the help of the thieves who had expropriated the USSR's wealth in the aftermath of her collapse and who had become the new aristocracy, Putin won the presidency, then again, and yet again.

Perhaps this is what drew the American Archie Bunker types who now support Trump to admire Putin in the first place, even before Trump started his campaign. A strongman leader not just promising the politics of restoration, but truly delivering it. There has long been a creepy affinity toward Putin's Russia from the main elements of the Trump coalition.

31

White evangelical Christians, NRA gun fetishists and the Fox/Breitbart white nationalists all seem to see in Putin's near exclusively white, anti-Muslim, anti-gay authoritarianism a model for our own country.

In any event, whatever love these folks have for the Russian near-dictator, it's pretty obvious that Putin is not interested in reciprocating. Rather, key to Making Russia Great Again is weakening America and, in particular, America's relationship with our traditional allies in Western Europe, Japan, South Korea and so on. For Russia to prosper and increase her influence in world affairs, the United States' partnerships with these nations would have to weaken.

So when Trump entered the Republican primary in the summer of 2015, Putin found himself with the opportunity of a lifetime. For a relatively small investment, he was not only able to block the woman he hated from becoming the American president, but he put in place a cartoonish egomaniac who is not only unwilling, but obviously unable to carry out the most basic duties of the highest office in the world's remaining superpower.

With Trump, Putin could not have gotten a more willing partner in the Oval Office if he had trained one from a young age and infiltrated him into the country, spy-novel style.

The president of the United States, from the campaign trail and continuing into the West Wing, has repeatedly (and falsely) claimed that NATO and the European Union have been cheating American taxpayers for decades, even going so far as claiming that the EU was created solely for that purpose. Trump did exactly zero to punish Russia for seizing three Ukrainian ships and crews in the Azov Sea off Crimea. For that matter, he has essentially taken Putin's side on the question of his invasion and annexation of that peninsula, at first merely blaming it all on Obama but eventually actively adopting Putin's claims that the residents there prefer Russian rule. He announced his sudden withdrawal from Syria without consulting our allies or even our own military leaders, essentially handing over the region to a Putin surrogate. To justify it, he claimed –

32

astonishingly – that Russia's aim was to defeat ISIS, and he was happy to have Putin take over that task for us. When Putin's agents tried to murder a defector and his daughter in London, Trump resisted imposing sanctions. After he was pressured into it, he got mad when he found out that the United States was expelling the same number of Russian "diplomats" as the entire European Union combined, not the number from each country individually, as he had believed.

Following a pair of one-on-one meetings with Putin in Helsinki and Buenos Aires after which he refused to brief his own government about what exactly was said and agreed to, Trump even started spouting Russian propaganda, describing the Soviet Union's invasion of Afghanistan in 1979 as justified because terrorists from that country had been carrying out attacks in Russia. This mystified historians and Russia experts in this country – but matched perfectly the revisionist account Putin is working hard to spread over there.

Finally, Trump has repeatedly taken Putin's word over that of the United States intelligence agencies, which concluded that Russia was behind the theft of emails from the Democratic National Committee and Clinton campaign chairman John Podesta and the subsequent distribution of those stolen documents through Russia-friendly WikiLeaks. Nor would he accept the U.S. intelligence community's conclusion that Russia had conducted a large-scale propaganda campaign through social media to hurt Clinton and help Trump win the presidency. Never mind that the details have been spelled out in public statements from his own Office of the Director of National Intelligence, in private to him personally during the transition, and in court filings by special counsel Robert Mueller. Granted, in this instance Trump has a clear self-interest in pretending that Russia did not help him win, but his willingness to tarnish the reputation of American intelligence and the U.S. justice system is, like so much else about his presidency, unprecedented.

Trump's corps of enablers in and near the Republican Party call those criticisms unfair, and point to the sanctions imposed

33

on Russian officials during his administration and the arms that have been sent to Ukraine as proof that Trump has really been tougher on Russia than Obama was – a statement that Trump naturally parrots whenever he's pressed on the topic. Trump and his defenders, of course, make no distinction between actions Trump himself has supported and those that have been pushed by majorities of both Democrats and Republicans in Congress or the professional national security corps across the various agencies. Trump did not want additional sanctions against Russia to punish it for its efforts to help him win, but feared the political cost of vetoing legislation that required them. He wasn't really aware of the arms sales, and he certainly had nothing to do with the deaths of dozens of Russian mercenaries in Syria at the hands of U.S. and allied forces, something his defenders frequently point to as proof of Trump's confrontational approach to the Russian autocrat.

No, if Trump has truly been tough on Russia, that would be news to our Western European allies, who have watched in stunned amazement while Trump repeatedly disparages them and speaks fondly of Putin. Indeed, how Trump has frayed those alliances has been Putin's greatest victory in geopolitical affairs. Trump as president has bad-mouthed and attacked both the North Atlantic Treaty Organization as well as the European Union, the two post-war structures that were largely founded by the United States as a way to end intra-Europe conflicts that had sparked two world wars in just 25 years. Trump accused them both of cheating the United States, even discussed withdrawing from NATO entirely, weakening both entities and in the process accomplishing Putin's top foreign policy objective since taking power. Putin has made no secret he would like Russia to return to Soviet-era dominance; an end to Western European unity makes that goal a lot easier.

Why Trump has been doing this is beyond the scope of this book. But regardless of the reason, it is plain that Vladimir Putin got more than he could ever have dreamed of as the election results rolled in from Florida, Pennsylvania, Michigan and Wisconsin.

Did he know Trump was going to win? Of course not. In fact, he probably assumed – like everybody else – that the election would wind up relatively close, that Trump would lose, and that he would make a huge fuss about how it had somehow been "rigged" and the presidency stolen from him. Such noise would help Trump's public profile and the TV network he was considering launching – but it would create a nightmare for President-elect Hillary Clinton as she set about naming her transition team amid daily protests and continued coverage in right-wing media about the "questions" Trump was raising regarding the legitimacy of the election.

And that, right there, is the whole point of Putin's interference from the start: To generate chaos. To break things. To make a giant, stinking mess. To have a significant chunk of the electorate in the world's erstwhile bastion of democracy questioning the integrity of basic governance would go a long way toward cutting us down to size. The likely assumption was that all of this would happen in a Hillary Clinton presidency, thereby weakening her on the world stage.

Imagine his glee when, against all the odds, he got Donald Trump instead. If chaos was his main objective, with Trump in the Oval Office, he has gotten that in spades.

~ ~ ~

There was a time, not terribly long ago, when the idea of an American president siding with Russia's dictator over his own intelligence agencies, over our western allies, over nations that had actually been invaded by him, would have raised holy hell in the Republican Party. That president would have been labeled a coward, an appeaser, a modern-day Neville Chamberlain – and those are just the printable things.

Instead, it is the Republican Party that was responsible for putting this man into power, and the response from its leaders has been a shrug, or even – astonishingly – a full-throated defense.

Right there, in fact, is a key word: "responsible." It's one that has gone missing from one of our two major political parties. Because as a major party, Republicans had a responsibility, indeed, an obligation, to protect America from someone so patently unready for the nation's highest office. They failed us miserably.

Maybe this was the natural consequence of cultivating a base more interested in keeping America white and Christian than the values it professed through the decades like limited government and freedom. The Republican Party was literally founded to abolish slavery. Its first president was assassinated because of his success in doing so, and for the next hundred years it remained on the side of civil rights and equal opportunity for minorities.

But ever since 1968, party leaders and candidates for national office have been willing to trade away that legacy for the sake of winning. What Trump did was simply take their strategy and crank up the volume. He tossed aside the dog whistle the party had been using for decades and replaced it with a bullhorn.

And while the party's failure to take its responsibility in this republic seriously has saddled both it and America with Trump, it's the Republican Party's future that is far more threatened. Trump's mob-boss-like insistence on personal loyalty has destroyed the party as an institution based on principles, and has replaced it with a personality cult. In as little as a few months but no longer than four and a half years, that personality goes away.

What then? How will the party regroup? There are no other pretend billionaires with near 100-percent name ID who are also willing to play along with racists and white nationalists. Yet that is the party Trump will have left.

No one in party leadership today seems remotely ready to deal with that inevitable scenario.

~ ~ ~

The clouds were threatening rain, which frankly would not have made things any more damp in the sticky humidity. Nevertheless, most of the Americans on the tarmac at Noi Bai International Airport outside of Hanoi were in business attire – the men in coats and ties, the women in heels and blazers.

There were several dozen there, walking the grounds, inspecting the marks where the nose wheels on Air Force One would stop, where the limo would pull up, where the press riser would be built. They worked for the advance teams from the White House Communications Agency, the Secret Service, the State Department, the Pentagon, and on and on. All of them, working their tails off, sweating through their clothes to prepare for a summit between Donald Trump and Kim Jong Un. Not because a major breakthrough on North Korea's nuclear weapons program had been reached or was even close enough that all it needed was a few minor tweaks for the two leaders to compromise upon. No, the summit was happening because Trump had just gotten spanked by new House Speaker Nancy Pelosi on Trump's pet issue of the border wall back home. Trump demanded a public relations "win" at any cost, and Kim was one of the few people in the world who at least pretended as if he liked him.

All of this effort, hundreds of men and women in Hanoi for the better part of a month, pulled from postings from Washington to Berlin to Canberra and every place in between, costing tens of millions of taxpayer dollars, all so a temperamental narcissist could come halfway around the world and say random nonsense.

Every once in a while these past few years, I've broken away from my train of thought at that moment and realized, yet again, that the president of the United States was, in fact, that same ridiculous egomaniac bragging about his ceiling molding and chandeliers at Mar-a-Lago. The first time was the day of the inauguration, seeing the TV shot of Trump climbing aboard a plane with the words "United States of America" painted on the side. I've felt it more than once seeing the White House at night, all lighted up in the darkness, thinking of the history and majesty of the place – before realizing, oh yeah, and its occupant is Donald J. Trump. I've felt it walking up the drive and past the West Wing entrance, seeing the Marine standing at attention by the door, and thinking – yeah, the president he is guarding is Donald J. Trump.

I had that same realization on the concrete apron in front of the VIP terminal at Hanoi airport – all of this time and effort and money so that Donald J. Trump could come satisfy a whim. We all knew that regardless of what was or was not agreed to in Hanoi, Trump would claim it as a major accomplishment, worthy of the Nobel Peace Prize, and certainly a justification for his re-election.

Yet .... all of this machinery of the state is, perhaps, the most comforting evidence that the nation will survive this – that the republic is strong enough to withstand an aberration even as deviant as the Trump presidency. Except for the handful of political hires among that contingent on the Hanoi tarmac, every one of the others would likely have done their jobs the exact same way had it been President Marco Rubio or President John Kasich or President Hillary Clinton. From the Defense Department to State to the civil servants who staff key White House support positions, we have an immense bureaucracy that is resistant to change. Even some political hires, after getting to understand the agencies they were brought in to upend, wind up appreciating the wisdom in the system and are effectively co-opted.

We are a massive container ship, plowing along steadily, regardless of who is at the helm. Even the most forceful and engaged presidents can only change course a few degrees over the span of two terms in office.

Often – too often – the bureaucracy is criticized as terrible and wasteful. Perhaps. But if America is to get through the Trump years, it will also be our salvation.

3. A Creature of the Tabloids

It happens pretty much every time Donald J. Trump, president of the United States of America, putative leader of the free world, opens his mouth, whether it's at a Cabinet meeting or a campaign rally or, most notably of late, from the podium of a coronavirus briefing. All over the nation, indeed, the planet, heads shake in amazement and the question arises yet again: How in the hell did this possibly happen?

One barely coherent sentence after another, each filled with angry bile toward his critics or unironic self-congratulations or a mixture of both but in either case completely woven through with absurd exaggerations and outright lies. How can this man actually be commander-in-chief?

In a particularly unhinged performance in March 2019, Trump claimed his election was bigger and more historic than Andrew Jackson's ("We had the greatest election!"). He re-litigated his false claims – two years later! – that he had had more people at his inaugural than Barack Obama had drawn in 2009. He lied about the crime rate of illegal immigrants. He misrepresented how tariffs work and who pays them. He took credit for the passage of the Veterans "Choice" program even though it had passed Congress two years before he was elected, and boasted of economic successes like the massive return of manufacturing jobs from overseas that have not happened. He even invented revisionist explanations of events like his call for Russia to steal Hillary Clinton's emails – despite there being video proof to the contrary.

Those, by the way, are just the highlights. A detailed accounting of his two-hour, four-minute, four-second speech to the Conservative Political Action Conference would require a separate appendix, if not its own volume. Of course, two years and five weeks into his presidency, with such gibberish coming on a near-daily basis, his remarks that afternoon barely raised an eyebrow.

Even the insane, and deadly, medical advice he delivered from the James S. Brady Briefing Room on April 23, 2020, about injecting disinfectants as a way to treat coronavirus was greeted by many with an oh-well-that's-just-Trump shrug.

Now, there are structural reasons why any major party nominee starts with at least a 45 percent chance of winning the presidency, perhaps even slightly higher if that nominee is of the opposite party from that of a term-limited incumbent. So once Trump had the nomination in hand, there was always the very real possibility he would become president, regardless of the polling at any given moment.

The bigger, lesser explored question is how this sort of person could have been taken seriously enough by enough adult human beings to win a major party nomination in the first place. Because Trump was not merely a bad candidate in the way Bob Dole or Michael Dukakis were bad candidates. If Dole had won in 1996 or Dukakis in 1988, the republic would have been fine. Both men had proven leadership skills in difficult jobs. In stark contrast, Trump was not merely a difference in degree but in kind. There was absolutely nothing in his background that suggested he was qualified for the job, and quite a bit to suggest that he would be an unmitigated disaster. If Donald J. Trump went to the airport and demanded to fly your airliner or showed up at an operating room wanting to perform your heart surgery, he would rightly be escorted off by security. Yet throwing his name in for a job that carries far more responsibility than either? He was welcomed in as a reasonable prospect.

What? How?

Amazingly to some, predictably to others, the answers to those questions lie in the tabloid gossip capital of the universe in the 1980s and 1990s – otherwise known as Manhattan.

~ ~ ~

One summer day in 1991, a man named John Miller called up a reporter at *People* magazine with a juicy tip. His boss, the famous multi-billionaire real estate mogul and playboy Donald Trump, was having a fling with one of the hottest new supermodels of the day, Carla Bruni. Miller told the reporter on condition of anonymity that, with Trump's marriage to Ivana over, his boss was in no rush to settle down with girlfriend Marla Maples; that, in fact, Maples was pretty much done, too, and that he had three girlfriends, not counting Bruni or the overtures coming to him from Madonna and Kim Basinger, and that The Donald was back on the market.

As it happens, almost none of what Sue Carswell was told on the phone that day was true.

Trump may have wished his relationship with Maples was over, but he hadn't had the guts to tell Maples that yet. He absolutely was not having sex with Bruni – when she was asked about the claim, she answered that she didn't even know him and that he was a lunatic. The other name-drops were also aspirational, at best. But the most spectacular, most outrageous lie of the whole incident? There was no John Miller. There was only Trump, inventing and using a pseudonym for himself to plant a fake story designed.... to what end, exactly?

Clearly, falsely claiming he was sleeping with an Italian model was not going to persuade her into doing so. Perhaps he was hoping Maples would see the article and move out, saving him a difficult conversation?

That we're even at these second-order questions is testament to what a twisted individual we have given the honor of being our president. What sort of person *does* this stuff?

The sort of person, as it turns out, who does really well in "reality television" – which anyone familiar with the genre

41

knows, really has nothing to do with reality at all. "Reality" shows do not explore real-world problems. They don't have "real" people in them, or at least real in any normal sense of the word. Rather, what they do is create situations where somewhat normal people (with the caveat that they have *chosen* to appear in this type of programming, thereby casting serious doubt on their claims to normalcy) are put in situations where truly manipulative, even mean-spirited behavior is the most handsomely rewarded.

Naturally, it was exactly this medium that put Trump in a position where a candidacy for the presidency was practicable, despite his complete lack of qualifications. Because Trump's role in "The Apprentice" was not merely as a contestant who would appear in a single season of episodes. Rather, he was the show's sole continuing thread through the years. Yes, he acted like a jerk on the show – ridiculing, browbeating and otherwise mistreating characters (which was not, as we have now learned, really "acting" at all). Far more important, from the standpoint of how things wound up shaking out, was the character he got to play: A shrewd, self-made billionaire used to making important business decisions that affected the lives of many thousands of employees across the globe.

In real-life reality, not a single one of those character traits is accurate. Trump inherited his wealth, and basically treaded water through the years to more or less be in the same place financially that he was on the day he took over his father's company in 1974. Despite his grandiose claims of having tens of thousands of employees all over the world under the umbrella of the Trump Organization, in truth his company was never more than a small family business, which became even smaller after the failure of his Atlantic City casinos essentially left him running golf course resorts and licensing his last name to put on other people's buildings.

None of this mattered. From attendees of his big, WrestleMania-like rallies to supposedly sophisticated mega-donors to the Republican Party, Trump had them all fooled. His "reality" show image had become reality, for millions and

42

millions and millions of Americans. It was a long con, perpetrated over decades.

~ ~ ~

Long before the Internet made stupid readily available to anyone with a smart phone, it was a major perk of living in the Big Apple. There, for just a couple of quarters, you could pick up one of two daily tabloids that made it their business to seek out and print salacious and trivial nonsense about movie stars, sports stars, rich people and other celebrities, even those celebrated just for being celebrated.

It is true that many other cities, especially Los Angeles, had a celebrity culture and gossip columnists and so forth, but none could compete with New York, particularly given the continual battle for dominance between the two newspapers.

People who never lived in New York in those years may not appreciate what the tabs delivered, or even what "tabloid" refers to. Unlike the *New York Times* and the *Wall Street Journal* that were printed on large sheets of newsprint that you pretty much needed a desk or table to read comfortably, the *Daily News* and the *New York Post* were published on sheets small enough to read them on the subway or the bus. The *Times* and certainly the *Journal* were written for people who made money with other people's money. The *News* and the *Post* were written for people who worked for a living.

And, as it turned out, what people who worked for a living loved to learn about was who was buying what crazy expensive penthouse apartment where, who had just been secretly married in St. Bart's with only their closest 500 friends in attendance, who was having extramarital sex with whom, and what was going to happen when the wife found out.

This is not to diminish the local government and sports reporting and writing of the *News* and the *Post*, particularly the *News*. It was first-rate, and – to be honest – could be understood on the first pass, as opposed to the triple-nested-clause sentences preferred by the *Times*. Nevertheless, the most well-read sections in both were often the gossip pages, especially the notorious Page Six, with the material frequently moved to the front page, when it seemed like it offered the best shot of goosing that day's newsstand sales – that era's version of "click bait."

This is not, of course, the turf that the truly wealthy wish to play on. Seriously rich people, or at least the grownups among them, have little use for being named in the scandal sheets and society pages. Many of the most successful people in business have managed to become and remain successful without getting their personal affairs splashed across the New York City tabs even once, and that's how they have preferred it.

Not so, Donald J. Trump, from Jamaica Estates, Queens. The honestly wealthy real estate titans of New York cherished their privacy and loathed when some tidbit about an appearance at a gala or a reception made the gossip pages. But for Trump, even the smallest media mention was yet more proof that he, a child of the builder of government-subsidized homes for the bridge-and-tunnel crowd, had finally made it.

The more he was featured in those pages, the more important he obviously must be, regardless of the impression any particular story might leave with a normal person. Hence, when first wife Ivana got the *Daily News* to print her side of the divorce tale on its cover, a furious Trump called the *Post* to get on *their* cover – resulting in the now famous "BEST SEX I'VE EVER HAD" headline.

Getting into these pages was not really difficult for him. These columns had to run every single day, which meant the columnists were always scrounging for fodder. Calling Trump's office was good for an easy item, even if it meant having to pretend that you didn't recognize that John Miller or John Barron was in fact Trump himself – or if what you printed wound up being patently false. Like the time Trump planted "news" that Prince Charles was going to buy units at Trump Tower.

The key point here is that in most of this nonsense coverage, the shorthand descriptor for Trump was "billionaire real estate mogul." Never mind that his big "deals" often fell apart or never happened at all. So while typical New Yorkers might have been skeptical about the claims of his sexual prowess or most recent supermodel conquest, they had little reason to doubt the more fundamental lie about his great wealth and its origins.

And it was this piece of fiction, generally accepted as fact, that begat everything else.

~ ~ ~

In 1985, Random House wanted to do a billionaire book. It was the second half of the Reagan presidency, and the very rich were enjoying a period of extraordinary worship, beyond even the normal American fascination with wealth. Random was owned by the company that also owned Condé Nast, which included *GQ*, which had happened to do a cover story on Trump the previous year.

That piece had generated unusually high newsstand sales. Publisher Si Newhouse smelled a winner, and approached Trump about an autobiography. Trump naturally was thrilled with the idea and agreed to a half million dollar advance. Of course, Trump writes about as much as he reads – which is to say, almost not at all – and therefore needed a ghostwriter.

Enter Tony Schwartz, a reporter for *New York Magazine* who had profiled Trump previously and who happened to be in his office hoping to interview him for a follow-up when Trump out of the blue asked if he would ghostwrite a book in exchange for half the advance and royalties.

And thus was born the next step in the creation myth of Donald Trump, stupendously successful businessman: *The Art of the Deal*.

As Schwartz explained in 2016 to *The New Yorker's* Jane Mayer, the title was his idea, as was the structure … as was the voice … and, most important, the choice to draw Trump as far more engaged, knowledgeable and empathetic than he actually was. Schwartz said he realized that portraying Trump accurately would not help book sales. Readers want a likeable protagonist. So he invented one.

Starting, in fact, from the book's very first lines: "I don't do it for the money," Schwartz wrote. "I've got enough, much more than I'll ever need. I do it to do it. Deals are my art form. Other people paint beautifully on canvas or write wonderful poetry. I like making deals, preferably big deals. That's how I get my kicks."

Three decades later, Schwartz told *The New Yorker* that nothing could be further from the truth: "Of course he's in it for the money…. One of the most deep and basic needs he has is to prove that 'I'm richer than you.'"

Schwartz became one of Trump's most strident critics upon the start of his presidential campaign, warning anyone who would listen that Trump was completely unfit for the job. He had made millions from the book, but now disavowed it as fiction. "I put lipstick on a pig," he told Mayer. "I feel a deep sense of remorse that I contributed to presenting Trump in a way that brought him wider attention and made him more appealing than he is."

Schwartz was, of course, correct. Previously, Trump's fan base largely had been limited to the circulation area of the *New York Daily News* and the *New York Post* – the five boroughs, Long Island, perhaps a portion of northern New Jersey. *The Art of the Deal* spread this virus across the country and even around the world. The book spent nearly a year on the *New York Times* bestseller list, with three months of that at the very top.

The great irony is that the book came out just a couple of years before Trump's self-proclaimed Midas touch proved out to be more of a leaden curse. Trump went on a spending orgy, buying up the Plaza Hotel in midtown Manhattan, a troubled airline, a string of Atlantic City casinos and the 281-foot "Trump Princess" motor yacht. It was not long before all of those choices proved unwise, even reckless. Journalist David Cay Johnston found a financial statement from 1990 that showed Trump's net worth was negative $300 million.

Trump had vastly overpaid for the Plaza. The "Trump Shuttle" airline lost millions under his dubious stewardship, which included a crash landing in Boston. Amazingly, he defied the laws of probability and mathematics by losing even more millions on his casinos and running them into bankruptcy. And while any boat is a hole in the water into which you throw money, a 281-foot boat makes for a really deep hole.

The bankruptcy filings – the first in 1991; six in all – led to a new reality for Trump. The banks forced him to unload the hotel, the airline, the yacht and the jetliner he owned for his personal use. That he survived at all is a testament to his shamelessness: He basically argued that he was too big to fail, and that he'd drag the banks down with him if they cut him loose. That argument worked, to a degree. He did not have to declare personal bankruptcy, but he did have to live on an allowance (albeit one that 99.99 percent of Americans would happily take: $450,000 per month) and the days of finding willing lenders for his deals were over.

And that could have been the end of Donald J. Trump as a human being the rest of the planet had to care about, if not for a new and even more base version of tabloid gossip that was taking root by the end of the last century: "reality" television.

~ ~ ~

As big a bestseller as *The Art of the Deal* was, only a tiny percentage of Americans had actually read it. That's hardly unusual. Most Americans don't read many books, and there are a great number of books published every year.

Fortunately for Trump, far exceeding the number of Americans who had read *The Art of the Deal* was the number of Americans who had heard something about it, and included in that category was former British paratrooper turned reality show impresario Mark Burnett. In 2002, Burnett had rented Wollman skating rink in New York's Central Park, which Trump had refurbished for the city some years earlier, for a broadcast of that season's finale of "Survivor."

For those lucky enough to have missed this program when it aired, it essentially lionized people for being more conniving, more manipulative, more ruthless – essentially, for being bigger jerks – than their fellow contestants, all set in some remote location and featuring bizarre competitions such as eating bugs. It was, naturally, a huge hit. Some 125 million Americans watched the final episode of the first season.

By 2002, Burnett was working on yet another idea: people competing against each other for a business reward. Basically Survivor again, only set in a corporate boardroom. As he spoke to the crowd of guests gathered to watch the broadcast, Burnett noticed Trump there in the front row, according to a 2019 *New Yorker* profile by Patrick Radden Keefe, and immediately started mentioning the word "Trump" as frequently as possible. Trump shook his hand afterward and told him he was a genius. Burnett told Trump that a passing roller-blader on Venice Beach years earlier had given Burnett a copy of *The Art of the Deal* and that it had changed his life. The outrageous flattery succeeded, of course, and Burnett had successfully cast the tycoon for his new show.

It would be called "The Apprentice," but it was basically "Corporate Survivor." The contestants were divided into teams and would compete to finish "business" challenges. The word "business" is in quotes because some of these tasks were about as meaningful as eating insect larvae. Buying and selling items at a flea market. Designing a pizza for Domino's and selling them from a trailer. Only instead of the contestants voting each other off the show, Trump himself would fire one contestant each week, until the winner would be rewarded with a one-year job working for the Trump Organization (one contestant reported to Keefe that the salary was in fact coming from NBC, not Trump.)

Trump co-produced the show with Burnett, which over the years put hundreds of millions of dollars in their pockets (and, on a side note, gave Trump control over the un-aired recordings made during the tapings, which reportedly have him saying untoward things about women and minorities). Possibly an even bigger benefit to Trump, though, was cementing a national image as a renowned businessman, able to make good, reasoned decisions that had earned him an astronomical amount of money over his career.

The makers of the program knew better, of course. They reported how the furniture at Trump Tower was old and battered, how local merchants refused to do business with them because of all the times Trump had stiffed them in the past, how Trump himself was so inattentive and unfocused that he would sometimes wind up firing someone in the end-of-episode "boardroom" scene who had done a perfectly fine job at that week's assigned task. Then it was up to the editors to go back through all the unused tape and find reasons to justify Trump's completely random decision.

"I find it strangely validating to hear that they're doing the same thing in the White House," show editor Jonathon Braun told *The New Yorker*, referring to the executive branch's frequent attempts to reverse-engineer a policy to match Trump's false statements.

The millions watching the program, however, knew none of that. To those unfamiliar with Trump's financial disasters in the 1990s, Trump was an unalloyed success. The first season, in particular, showcased one Trump property after another. Trump Tower was featured in every episode, as was Trump's Boeing 757 that he had bought to replace the 727 the banks had made him unload a decade earlier. Add in Trump's continuous self-promotion, and it's understandable why a lot of low-information voters saw in Trump perhaps the most successful businessman … ever.

For fourteen years this characterization was broadcast on national television, week after week, almost entirely unchallenged. The Trump creation myth that started in a single city but had then spread far and wide with *The Art of the Deal* became a downright national contagion thanks to The Apprentice.

It is difficult to overstate the consequences.

~ ~ ~

In the summer of 2016, the morning after a Trump campaign rally at a local college gym in St. Clairsville, Ohio, I visited the stereotypical down-on-its-luck downtown to talk to some locals outside of the hyper frenzy of Trump's carnival. Most people don't go to political rallies, and talking only to those who do gives a skewed perspective.

I spoke to people in a general store, a convenience store, a service station, at a community center's parking lot. What I heard was edifying. While Trump apologists have tried their best to sell the "economic anxiety" theme as the reason why he won places that had been historically Democratic, I did not hear much of that at all. Rather, it was mainly "cultural" conservatism driving their views on Trump. He was going to end political correctness and bring back "traditional" values and end illegal immigration and on and on. In order words, the politics of "restoration" – making America like it was in the 1950s again.

I expected to hear that. What surprised me was their reason for why Trump would be able to do these things that other Republican presidents previously had not. It was, they told me, because Trump was a tremendous businessman, maybe the best businessman of all time, and he knew how to get things done.

In an old-fashioned barber shop, I tried to push a couple of the customers on this, pointing out Trump's checkered business history and multiple bankruptcies. One gentleman awaiting his turn said he still thought Trump would do what he said because business people understood what a promise meant.

When I pointed out the thousands of lawsuits against Trump over the years accusing him of reneging on signed contracts and suggested that maybe Trump might not even try to deliver on some of his promises, the proprietor turned toward me angrily, gesturing with his scissors: "Mister Trump is a man of his word!"

At the Republican National Convention in Cleveland, when I would ask big donors, people who were writing six-figure checks to the party to help Trump win, people who really were successful in business, why they believed Trump would do the things he said, they similarly would cite Trump's immense wealth and many successes over the years.

From tabloid fixture to television game show host to presidential nominee and now, commander-in-chief, Trump's singular talent through all of this has been an unrelenting shamelessness to say that he is the best, that no one has come close, and anyone who disagrees is a jealous liar.

~ ~ ~

That Trump achieved such fame based on so little substance and was able to inflict himself on the entire world thanks to New York's tabloid culture is, of course, bad enough. Unfortunately, that wasn't the only consequence of that symbiotic relationship.

Thanks to his many years of successfully lying to gossip writers desperate to fill column inches, Trump learned that there was no real downside to those dishonesties. The main reason for this, admittedly, was that he was fairly inconsequential. It did not matter what a second-rate real estate huckster said about properties he was trying to sell because the only ones who could be harmed were the ones buying his overpriced units. Similarly, whom Trump was claiming to be having sex with versus whom Trump was actually having sex with was of no real consequence to the republic.

Nevertheless, because Trump has always had an outsized opinion of himself, the lesson he appears to have drawn from those years is that he possesses some mystical property that allows him to get away with anything – to say whatever he wants to whomever he wants, regardless of its veracity.

He essentially told exactly this to Billy Bush of Access Hollywood's "grab 'em by the pussy" fame: "People will just believe you. You just tell them and they believe you," Bush said Trump told him.

For the first months of his presidential campaign, Trump continued just saying whatever he felt like with relatively little push back from journalists covering the race. Other candidates and their staffs believed this was because reporters and producers wanted Trump to win, but the reality is much less nefarious. In truth, most reporters believed – as did most of the rival campaigns – that Trump had next to zero chance of winning, largely because his life history was completely crossways to the erstwhile values of Christian conservatives who dominate the GOP primary electorate. Reporters assumed that by autumn, the serious candidates would use their considerable financial advantages to demolish Trump in states like Iowa and South Carolina.

Television producers and hosts, meanwhile, saw Trump as a way to get through the lean months of 2015, when normal humans aren't really paying attention to a presidential election more than a year away. Trump would say ridiculous, outrageous things at his rallies – and that was a whole lot more entertaining than Jeb Bush's 10-point plans or Marco Rubio's hundredth retelling of his life story.

And then later, after Trump had clinched the nomination and had, therefore, a serious chance of becoming president, an entirely different framework took hold, once again redounding to Trump's benefit.

~ ~ ~

For decades, Republicans have successfully badgered the American media with false accusations that they are biased against their party. These complaints literally go back to the 1950s, but were really cranked up with the advent of Fox News in the 1990s.

GOP office-holders, candidates and consultants have aggressively attacked media outlets as favoring Democrats. Though most often ill-founded and in bad faith, too many reporters and editors have become hyper-sensitized, and have bent over so far backward in the name of "balance" as to become inaccurate.

So it was that when an ill-informed, ill-prepared con artist landed the Republican nomination, that simple truth was almost never expressed that plainly. Rather, the fact that Trump had won the nomination somehow became validation of Trump's bona fides and worthiness.

With Donald Trump, America got as the Republican nominee the id of an 11-year-old boy with severe emotional developmental issues. The hundreds of millions of dollars he was born to allowed him to advance chronologically, straight into old age, without ever having to grow up. Thus the silly insults, the puerile taunts, the tantrums, the constant attention-seeking.

Throughout the campaign, we were assured by Trump's inner circle that this was all an act. Part of his "Apprentice" persona he had used over the years to bully and cajole his way to tremendous success. In reality, we were told, Trump was reasonable and smart and made sound decisions.

This spin-job, of course, should have been the first warning sign. To anyone with access to Google and even five free minutes, it would be pretty obvious that whatever it was that Trump had bullied and cajoled his way into, tremendous success wasn't it. To the contrary, he had managed to hang onto some measure of the wealth his father had left him in spite of his intellectual capacity and business skills, not because of them.

Once he'd won the presidency and his behavior was on display each and every day, it became clear that "the act" was in reality on those rare occasions that Trump spoke and behaved like a normal grown up. Hearing tales of Trump's antics in the White House, actually seeing and listening to him up close, it was apparent within days of his taking the oath of office that America had elected someone profoundly ill-equipped to handle even the simplest challenges of the job.

Yet, how is this conveyed to Americans who don't have the time or the tools to see this first-hand, day after day? The term of art has been "norm-shattering."

53

Well, yes, this is technically correct in the same way that John Wayne Gacy was "norm shattering" in the annals of serial killers. But the phrase is terribly misleading, and does far more to obfuscate the truth than to illuminate it.

Trump's most ardent supporters claimed, after all, that they wanted him to shatter norms. Leave aside the majority of his hardest-core fans for the moment – the ones who supported Trump because he was openly appealing to racist and xenophobic fears, rather than just winking at them. The Trump voters who really did vote for Obama at least once and perhaps even for Sanders in the 2016 Democratic primary truly believe "the system" is broken, and therefore someone who comes in to topple it is doing a great service.

When the media shorthand for what Trump does is that he shatters norms, those voters not paying close attention – again: most voters – will see that as a good thing.

Of course, the reporters and editors who use that phrase don't mean that Trump came to Washington and began demanding transparency in "dark money" political donations and public financing of federal campaigns or an end to presidential big-dollar fundraisers. Those things, which would offend the political power structure of both parties, truly would shatter the norms of how Washington works.

Rather, what reporters and editors mean when they say Trump is "shattering norms" is that Trump is acting like an abusive jerk. Or a cranky toddler. Or a lazy teenager. Or, simply, bat-shit crazy.

The problem, obviously, is that journalism is not supposed to make characterizations like that or draw those sorts of conclusions. I understand that norm and have lived by it for three decades in places as small as the Middletown *Times Herald Record* in upstate New York and as large as the Associated Press and NPR.

Trump understands this. His White House understands this. And both have been taking advantage of mainstream journalists' deeply ingrained self-censorship to the fullest. Anyone who covers this White House or who covered Trump's campaign knows full well that the emperor is not wearing any clothes, but news coverage that attempts to convey that is immediately attacked as "Fake News" and anti-Trump bias.

In the case of the Russian interference in the election, the shorthand that came into common usage was "meddling." The Russians had "meddled" in our elections.

It happened in news conferences, when reporters would ask Trump if he had pressed Putin on the "election meddling," and Trump would answer that Putin had denied meddling, and what was Trump supposed to do, get in a fight with him?

The problem was that for Americans not paying close attention to the news – once again: that means *most* Americans – the word "meddling" has a minor and innocuous connotation that diminishes what happened. The Russians didn't come kick the plug out of the outlet on some voting machines or put super glue in the door locks at a few polling places.

No, what Vladimir Putin did was use his spy agencies to coordinate a sophisticated operation to help Donald Trump get elected president of the United States. They mounted an enormous propaganda campaign using paid Internet "trolls" in Russia to disseminate literal fake news attacking Clinton and boosting Trump, adopting fake America personae. They stole private emails from the DNC and Clinton's campaign chairman and then distributed them on the Internet using their agent, WikiLeaks, which Trump then cited and amplified every single day in his appearances during that crucial, final month of the election campaign.

This goes well beyond "meddling" – "rigging an election" is closer to the truth.

~ ~ ~

Most media outlets and most White House reporters have, in time, learned to adapt to Trump's serial dishonesties. Cable television started running chyrons pointing out his and his staff's falsehoods in real time. Fact-checkers have guaranteed job security for the duration of his presidency. And many print journalists, myself included, have taken to adding the fact of Trump's many falsehoods and, at times, provable lies relatively high in our articles as necessary context.

It goes without saying that this should not be necessary – and in every past presidential administration that I can recall, it has not been necessary. While Trump's apologists are quick with the "well, all politicians lie," this is not in fact true. What *is* true is that no politician likes media coverage that makes him look bad. This is why most politicians whose budgets will allow it hire media relations staff to try to generate as much positive press as possible and dissuade reporters from producing negative press. In the past, this has meant staffers calling up reporters and chewing them out about the structure or "angle" of a story. Sometimes the staffers might even have had a point.

But never, going back at least as far as the Richard Nixon years, has the White House press corps faced such brazen and repeated lies to our faces, combined with vicious personal attacks on our integrity. In fact, it was the opposite. Previous presidents and their staffs bent over backward to avoid openly lying because they believed that their credibility was the most valuable thing they possessed, and if they were to lose that, they could never get it back. They tried to wheedle and dodge and obfuscate – but did their damnedest not to say things they knew to be untrue.

Trump personally and much of his White House are completely different. They simply don't care whether what they say is true or false, because they appear to believe that the average American doesn't care about something as abstract as truth.

Of all the worrisome things from the Trump presidency, and there are many, this is probably the most corrosive to the fabric of a democracy. Truth matters, and the fact that the entire executive branch of the United States government is led by people who see reality as whatever the boss wants it to be at that moment should be more than a little troubling. This goes way beyond arguing about whether tax cuts pay for themselves or about the best policies to deal with climate change.

What Trump has done is create a literal cult dedicated to feeding and soothing an adolescent ego. What he did for himself with the New York gossip columnists using his fictional "John Miller" and "John Barron," he had Sean Spicer and Kellyanne Conway and Sarah Sanders and Kayleigh McEnany doing for him in the West Wing.

"Alternative facts," as Conway put them, are no such thing. They are lies. This is not about who Donald J. Trump is pretending he's having sex with or whether any British royals are buying his apartments. This is about our country and how it's being run.

The president, his staff, everyone in his administration, in fact, work for us. And we deserve better.

4. Nixon's Deal with the Devil

Sometimes you learn so much more about this world by just shutting up and listening.

All those illegals coming over, they know they'll get amnesty.

It was the Iowa State Fair, summer of 2015, near the queue for their straw poll – only, instead of filling out a ballot, you got a kernel of corn and dropped it into the jar labeled with the candidate you wanted as your next president.

Maybe not tomorrow, but someday.

At the booth at the head of the line, the jar with Ted Cruz's picture on it was maybe a third full. Jeb Bush's jar had a small pile of popcorn kernels at the bottom. Marco Rubio's jar was almost at the halfway point – but then right next to it, Donald Trump's jar was nearly full. The attendant had explained to me a little earlier that it had already been emptied four times that day.

And their kids! If they're born here, they're automatically citizens! And they all vote Democrat. You KNOW that's why they want 'em. We'll never get another Republican president again!

Yup. And Trump's the only one with the balls to stop 'em.

I had retreated to the shade of a tree to escape the August sun, but could hear the conversation clearly. They were both late middle age. Dark tans, jeans and T-shirts. It probably goes without saying, but the men were both white.

After they had deposited their kernels into Trump's jar, I hurried after them. They acknowledged their support for Trump and gave the usual reasons. He told it like it was. He wasn't politically correct. Great businessman. Couldn't be bought. I asked whether his views on immigration were at all important to them, and they shook their heads nonchalantly. No, not really.

I asked if I could get their names, but they politely declined and went their separate ways. As I cleaned up my notes on what I'd just witnessed, its import began to dawn on me. I had previously assumed that Trump's popularity had largely sprung from his novelty. While the other candidates visiting the fairgrounds in Des Moines were making serious speeches, eating random food items that had either been deep-fried or served on a stick or both, and touring the "butter cow" exhibit with appropriate reverence, Trump had been offering children rides on his personal helicopter.

But after listening to his supporters' unvarnished comments, I realized how his hold went way beyond mere entertainment value, and how he had co-opted the Frankenstein's monster of xenophobia, fear and outright racism that the Republican Party had built over the decades, but had tried to keep carefully tamed.

It was an eye-opening moment – and I understood straight away what a threat Trump posed to the party establishment.

~ ~ ~

When Lyndon Johnson signed the Civil Rights Act of 1964, he is said to have quipped that he was simultaneously signing over the South to the Republican Party for a generation.

Well, he was half right, or perhaps just a third. Because it's been more than 50 years now, two, getting on three generations, and Republicans still pretty much own the American South – at least in those areas where white people constitute the majority.

And *this*, of course, is the fundamental reason behind the rise of Trump. His takeover of the Republican Party did not happen in a vacuum.

The irony of this is sometimes lost on Americans today. After all, the Republicans became a party specifically to free the slaves. Abolitionism was its *raison d'etre*, and its first president, Abraham Lincoln, was murdered for having succeeded in that mission. During the first half of the last century, while Democrats were the entrenched party of the South – people would declare they would sooner vote for a yellow dog than a Republican – and spawning off "civic groups" like the Ku Klux Klan, it was the GOP that remained the home for progressive-minded advocates of civil rights for freed slaves and their descendants. Perhaps forgotten is that when LBJ managed to finagle the Voting Rights Act and the Civil Rights Act into law, it was not Republicans whose arms he had to twist the hardest, but those of enough southern Democrats to get them through Congress.

Yet it came to pass that Lincoln's party, the party that pushed long and hard for civil rights for African-Americans for the first two-thirds of the last century – a plurality of *that* party decided 153 years after the Emancipation Proclamation that the most openly racist candidate since George Wallace should be their choice to be president of the United States.

How that came to be is actually pretty simple. Because in those years that Johnson's legacy legislation was pushing southern Democrats away from the party that had stood behind their segregationism for nearly a hundred years, Richard Nixon was only too happy to welcome them aboard his new, improved Republican Party. This updated Grand Old Party was going to be for *states' rights* and *law and order* – phrases that those intended to hear them would understand exactly what had been meant by them.

It was dubbed the "Southern Strategy," and it was used by Nixon and his Republican presidential nominee successors in the coming decades with ruthless effect. From 1968 through 1988, Democrats were victorious in exactly one presidential election: Jimmy Carter's, in 1976, and only because the nation had been so traumatized by Watergate, Nixon's resignation, and his subsequent pardon by Gerald Ford.

In every one of their wins, Republicans successfully appealed to former Democrats in the South – and voters all over the country who thought like former Democrats in the South – with coded appeals that made it clear Republicans were on their side in this battle. Nixon's approach was to talk up "law and order." It did not have to be spoken aloud that his "silent majority" supporting this law and order were white people, as opposed to those Blacks and hippies who were always protesting and rioting and taking drugs. Ronald Reagan gave a speech backing "states' rights" near Philadelphia, Mississippi, site of the 1964 murders of the Freedom Summer activists. He also spoke of his (apocryphal) Cadillac-driving welfare queen; it went without saying that she was Black. And George H.W. Bush's people famously made the Willie Horton ad – which essentially told the target audience that if you voted for Michael Dukakis, a large Black man would come to your home to rape and kill your wife.

Bush, nevertheless, was primaried by conservative rabble-rouser Pat Buchanan in 1992. And while there's a lot of revisionism that plays up the role of Bush's reversal on his "no new taxes" pledge as the cause of his downfall, that was not Buchanan's big campaign message. Rather, it was a populist attack on "elites" who were allowing the nation to slip from the grasp of white Christians. His speech at the convention later that summer summed it up: America was under attack from these "others" and it would require a culture war to win it back.

Bush lost that November, in large part because reliably Republican California flipped to the Democrats. The root cause was shifting demographics, a phenomenon that would in the coming years also move New Mexico, Colorado and Nevada away from Republicans. Despite this, Republicans stuck with the tried-and-true, barely-veiled racial appeals. Their candidates continued to attack welfare and other government programs because of the (incorrect) presumption among a segment of white voters that the beneficiaries were mainly Black and Latino. George W. Bush, struggling in the primaries against John McCain, went to openly racist Bob Jones University and told the audience that he shared their values (his brother, Jeb, and sister-in-law, Columba, would have been expelled, had they been students there, for their interracial relationship) and defended the flying of the Confederate flag from the South Carolina statehouse.

All of those elections, though, were mere prologue for what happened in 2008. Bill Clinton liked to call himself the first Black president because of his support from African-Americans, and white southerners largely despised him, even though he was one himself. But when the first actual African-American won the Democratic nomination – well, that was simply cataclysmic, the inevitable consequence of Pickett's Failed Charge finally come home to roost.

~ ~ ~

It is hard to overstate the effect Barack Obama's election had on the Republican voting base. True, this was something that had long been feared, but it had been feared as a terrible thing that would happen someday, perhaps a generation or two away.

Something for the kids or grandkids to cope with. I was in a boatyard in southern Virginia that election night, and the mainly older, exclusively white yachties were horrified at the result. Two months later, at a bed and breakfast in Fernandina Beach, a wealthy suburb of Jacksonville, Florida, the white proprietors asked if I planned to watch the inauguration that day – making it plain that the expected answer was no.

This is difficult for people who have grown up in Washington, D.C., or New York or Los Angeles to appreciate. Republicans from the South and all over the country have tried over the years to whitewash the loathing that many of their voters felt about Obama's election. It had nothing to do with race, they argued. He was a liberal Democrat, and they thought his policies would be bad for the country.

This was, of course, a ridiculous tissue of fiction, and it fell apart within months of Obama taking office.

Obama's first task was to deal with the financial crisis, which he did using mainstream economic theory that involved a government stimulus package to get money into the economy

62

as well as bailouts to selected industries, including banking, to keep credit flowing and people working. Recall how actual progressives hated the idea of not throwing all the Wall Street bankers in jail, how they wanted radical transformation of the entire system – nationalizing the big banks – and how, to this day, they continue to be angry at Obama for not having pushed that.

It didn't matter. To the GOP base, the mainstream-ness of Obama's plan meant less than nothing. The stimulus was "Obama's" stimulus, and Obama was Black. As Charlie Crist learned with his hug, Obama's skin color was far more significant to Republican primary voters than the state of the economy. And if reaction to the stimulus offered the first clue about the nature of so much of the opposition to Obama, what happened when he pushed for his health care plan provided all the remaining proof necessary.

Recall, again, how angry the progressive wing of the Democratic Party was at Obama for failing to jam through some version of single-payer health care, or at least a government-administered option for those who wanted it. Instead, in the hopes of fulfilling his campaign promise of bringing the country together and working with Republicans, Obama got behind a health care plan that was originally crafted by the conservative Heritage Foundation and implemented in Massachusetts by a Republican governor. In fact, had Mitt Romney won the nomination and the presidency in 2008 – as he well might have – he likely would have implemented some form of that same plan without any of the ensuing fuss.

But in 2010, the grassroots Republican base decided the Affordable Care Act was a threat to their very way of life, as was the president seeking to enact it. This is an important point: There were a number of congressional Republicans who likely would have been fine with the legislation and fine with working with the new Democratic president but opted not to support it for fear of losing their seats in their next primary. A proliferation of "Tea Party" activists – coincidentally enough, many of them had been proponents of the Obama as Secret

Kenyan Muslim Theory during the 2008 campaign – were demanding that Republican lawmakers oppose Obama on everything, all the time, and especially on the health care law.

And, so, oppose him they did. It was congressional Republicans who labeled the ACA "Obamacare" as a term of derision. Note that it wasn't called Socialist Care or Big Government Care, which were the supposed reasons for opposing the plan, but Obamacare. *This policy was created by Barack Obama, who was, by the way, still Black.* After the 2010 midterms that saw Democrats lose control of the House and lose seats in the Senate, minority leader Mitch McConnell famously stated that his chief priority was to make Obama a one-term president.

Party orthodoxy was not merely that Obama was advocating bad policies. Rather, it was accepted as gospel that Obama was the most incompetent president ever to be elected to the Oval Office. He knew nothing. His advisers knew nothing. They were staggering from one disaster to the next, and the country would be lucky to survive his tenure.

That was what "the base" was clamoring to hear, and so they heard it from pretty much every single Republican Party official, from county commissioners straight up to major state governors and U.S. senators. For the party leadership, it was a way of putting out the message they knew their voters wanted to hear while leaving themselves a path to claim that, no, they did not oppose Obama because of the color of his skin, but because he simply wasn't up to the challenge.

It's unclear if even a single one of them truly believed that.

~ ~ ~

Of course, if any additional evidence of the motivation behind all the Obama loathing were necessary, it arrived soon enough in the accelerated spread of the absurd conspiracy theory about his birthplace.

These wild claims began during his campaign against John McCain in 2008, but really took hold in 2010 and 2011, as

Republican base voters seemed to grow ever more incensed with each passing day that saw a Black man running the White House. It was ludicrous on its face. A hospital and public officials in Hawaii would have had to falsify a birth certificate, while coordinating with local newspapers to run a birth announcement, in order to invent an American provenance for a child who would decades later run for president.

It defies credulity to suggest that the basis for this accusation was anything other than the obvious one. Lots of candidates have run for president. How many of the previous ones were asked to produce birth certificates? In fact, in the 2008 election cycle, there actually *was* a candidate who was not born in the United States: John McCain, the Republican nominee. But did the "birthers" go after him? Of course not. Indeed, his colleagues in the U.S. Senate (including one Barack Obama) rightly passed a resolution declaring that his birth in the Panama Canal Zone where his Navy officer father had been stationed did not in any way prevent him from serving as president.

Amazingly, the racist wing of the GOP felt so emboldened in those years that it became a litmus test to ask elected Republicans whether they believed Obama was truly born in the United States. The most craven ones agreed that it was a legitimate question that needed investigating. The somewhat less craven ones would answer that they took the president at his word. And, to their credit, a significant percentage of Republican officials called the question ridiculous and refused to participate any further in the discussion.

Alert readers will remember which category Obama's successor – the current president of the United States, a Mr. Donald J. Trump of Queens, New York, who was still hosting his TV game show but making regular appearances on Fox News as a political expert – enthusiastically slotted himself into.

~ ~ ~

In the spring of 2011, Obama decided enough was enough and released a copy of his birth certificate. That put an end to most of the birther nonsense except for the true dead-enders who insisted that it was a forgery. (Yes, in fact, that group did include the current president of the United States.)

Of course, merely losing that particularly nutty line of attack did not end the racial animus and the white "anxiety" about losing "their" country to The Others. And so, predictably, the battle for the Republican nomination for the opportunity to challenge Obama quickly became a battle for who could prove they disliked immigrants the most.

Through the summer and fall of 2011, the Republican candidates had to outdo each other to show how tough they would be on illegal immigration in order to please the nativist "Tea Party" wing of their voting base. Most of them supported building a fence along the border with Mexico, or deploying the National Guard, or both. Minnesota congresswoman Michele Bachmann promised to build a fence along "every inch" of the Mexican border. Herman Cain of 9-9-9 tax policy fame even proposed electrifying the fence, although he later claimed he was only kidding (before changing his mind and saying that maybe he wasn't kidding after all). The candidates had to explain or, preferably, renounce their previous support for such things as issuing drivers licenses for undocumented immigrants or providing in-state college tuition to their children. When Texas Governor Rick Perry, following up on his apostasy of not supporting a full border fence, said "you don't have a heart" if you cannot empathize with children of undocumented immigrants, he was booed. And so it came to pass that former Massachusetts Governor Mitt Romney said from a debate stage that, yes, he was indeed going to be tough on illegal immigration. So tough, in fact, that people here illegally would choose to "self deport."

Looking back on it now, the threat seems mildly amusing. He wasn't calling them rapists and drug dealers. He wasn't promising a "Deportation Force" to kick them out. He said that his policies would be so harsh – presumably part of being "severely conservative," as he described himself at one point – that undocumented immigrants would decide they were better off leaving.

At the time, though, it was a big, big deal. Romney wasn't some raving nativist from the fringe like Tom Tancredo in 2008 or a retread desperate for publicity like Newt Gingrich. He was the odds on favorite to win the nomination. What he said mattered for the party as a whole.

Republicans understood that they were not going to make many inroads into the Black community running against the first Black president – while also understanding that they were picking up some white voters who ordinarily might have supported a Democrat or might not have voted at all except for the fact that the president was Black. But they were also aware that they needed a decent percentage of Latino voters to win – about 40 percent, and were nervous that the immigrant bashing and xenophobia of the primaries was going to hurt them in November, and that Romney's "self-deport" comment was going to be remembered.

As it turns out, their concern was well-informed.

~ ~ ~

Romney in the end did lose, which for a number of reasons was devastating to the national party.

Of note, however, was that he did not lose in the South. If the 2012 election had been conducted only among the eleven states that had formed the Confederacy, Romney would have won in a landslide – 118 electoral votes to Obama's 42.

The converse of this, though, is even more noteworthy. Among the non-Confederate states, Barack Obama won 290 electoral votes to Romney's 88.

What was obviously problematic for Republicans was that more and more states were becoming less and less white. And as the demographics shifted, so did voting patterns. Obama won North Carolina in 2008, and almost won it again in 2012. He won Florida both times and happened to be at the helm as both

New Mexico and Colorado became reliably Democratic, at least in presidential elections. More worrisome still were states that were voting Republican but could easily flip within a decade: Arizona, Texas, even Georgia. Were that to happen, the GOP would no longer be a national organization, but a regional party of the deepest South. It would never again win a presidential election.

Romney's loss, far more than McCain's four years earlier, set off deafening klaxons on the RNC bridge. McCain had gotten swamped in fundraising, in media attention. Everyone knew by October his race was pretty much over. Romney's campaign was another matter. He was competitive financially. His was a far better organized operation than McCain's. And as October ended, the anecdotal observations of crowd size were promising. Heading into election day, Republican Party leaders honestly believed they were going to win.

His loss, and a fairly solid loss, coming despite his performance in the South, therefore left the party elders in shock. Romney was a decent candidate, with plenty of money, against an incumbent hobbled by a still-soft economy and who was, by the way, African-American. And he *still* lost?

The Southern Strategy had failed them, and it was only going to become even less effective with each passing election.

~ ~ ~

Officially its name was the "Growth and Opportunity Project," created in the weeks following the election to analyze what had gone wrong and to put forth a plan to fix it in time for 2016, but everyone just called it "The Autopsy." Exit polling had shown precisely how badly Romney had done with Latino voters compared to previous GOP candidates, particularly George W. Bush, whose re-election campaign in 2004 wound up giving him 44 percent. McCain four years later saw that number fall to 31 percent. Romney won just 27 percent.

The authors, tellingly, included both Ari Fleischer, George W. Bush's former press secretary, and Sally Bradshaw, former

68

Florida Governor Jeb Bush's first chief of staff and longtime confidante. Jeb had married a Mexican native, had lived in Venezuela as a young man and was fluent in Spanish. He had never liked the nativist/racist wing of his party and was considering a run for the presidency himself in 2016.

The report came back within a couple of months, and was remarkable for its conclusions about the party's problem with minorities, which read as if they could have been written by the Brookings Institution or even the Center for American Progress.

"Republicans have lost the popular vote in five of the last six presidential elections," the report said. "States in which our presidential candidates used to win, such as New Mexico, Colorado, Nevada, Iowa, Ohio, New Hampshire, Virginia, and Florida, are increasingly voting Democratic. We are losing in too many places."

While it had some recommendations related to nuts and bolts campaign issues – the need for a better voter database; the wisdom of deploying field staff into swing states early – the heart of the report was the party's dismal image with non-white voters, and Latinos in particular.

"The nation's demographic changes add to the urgency of recognizing how precarious our position has become," the report stated. "According to the Pew Hispanic Center, in 2050, whites will be 47 percent of the country while Hispanics will grow to 29 percent and Asians to 9 percent."

Interestingly, Romney's campaign was the least "Southern Strategy" Republican campaign to date. What appeals it made to race were tangential. Romney primarily spoke to the wealthy and the near wealthy, meaning mainly white people, but it was not out of animus. That was his background. That was who he was. Of course, no blatant appeal to race was necessary, insofar as his opponent was the first Black president – but credit where credit is due. For example, McCain running mate Sarah Palin four years earlier was running against the first Black major party nominee, but that didn't prevent her from not just reaching for the old playbook, but reading aloud from it with gusto.

Nevertheless, Romney was the one who had just lost, and so he bore the brunt of the criticism.

"If we want ethnic minority voters to support Republicans, we have to engage them and show our sincerity," the report authors wrote. "If Hispanics think we do not want them here, they will close their ears to our policies."

At the Republican National Committee's summer meeting in Boston that August, chairman Reince Priebus was unsparing in his analysis of Romney's insensitivity toward Latinos. "Using the word 'self-deportation' — I mean, it's a horrific comment to make," he said. "It's not something that has anything to do with our party. But when a candidate makes those comments, obviously it hurts us."

Readers who skipped ahead a bit can already appreciate the irony. Yes, this would be the same Reince Priebus who failed to block Donald Trump's roll through the Republican primaries and then wound up serving as Trump's first chief of staff in the White House.

But at the time, the party leaders – the political staff as well as the 168 elected committee members from the states and territories – made a good faith effort to implement the report. The RNC recruited staff to set up shop in heavily Latino neighborhoods in key states and congressional districts heading into the 2014 midterms, with the intention of staying there through 2016. Party officials talked up outreach and talked down illegal immigration.

It's important to remember what a dramatic course change this was at the time. The demographic analysis alone, which pointed out how the United States would become a majority-minority country by 2050, and how the party would continue losing national elections if it did not make major reforms and make them immediately, was astounding to read in a Republican Party publication. This was essentially a complete repudiation of the party's Southern Strategy, a public *mea culpa* for years of ignoring minority voters and a sincere promise to do better.

And then self-proclaimed billionaire and voice of the common man Donald J. Trump rode down his escalator and talked about immigrant rapists and drug dealers and building a wall and making Mexico pay.

He might as well have taken the party's "Growth and Opportunity Project" report, set it on fire, and then stood over it, peeing on the flames.

~ ~ ~

Priebus and the other party leaders, in truth, were aghast. They had spent all this time and effort to show how Republicans had changed and were now really, truly interested in minority voters and along comes Trump and does *this*?

Of course, being upset by Trump and being able or even willing to try to do something about it were entirely different things. Trump was not really a Republican, and party leadership was genuinely worried that if they chased him off, he would simply run as an independent using his own money and siphon off a great bloc of votes from the eventual GOP nominee.

They were wrong about the first part. To run an effective independent campaign, Trump would have had to spend hundreds of millions of his own dollars, something that anyone who spent even ten minutes on Google would have realized was not going to happen because Trump was nowhere near as rich as he pretended to be.

But on the second point, they were sort of correct. In fact, the more openly racist things Trump said, the higher he rose in the polls. Indeed, that such a significant percentage of GOP primary voters took to Trump and stuck with him revealed exactly what they were really all about.

Priebus made an effort to get Trump to tone it down. And, naturally, Trump was not remotely interested in doing so. He has shown during his campaign and his presidency that he knows next to nothing about macroeconomics, international trade, modern aviation, American history, world history – just

71

to name a few. He does, understand, though, what white racists want to hear and what they don't want to hear.

He knew damned well that Barack Obama was born in Hawaii, but he pushed the "birther" conspiracy theory hard for years. He was, in fact, the nation's highest profile "birther," happily willing to lie to advance the slander. In 2011, he claimed on NBC's Today Show that he had sent investigators to Hawaii to look into the matter. "I have people that have been studying it and they cannot believe what they're finding," he said on national television.

Asked later what, exactly, his "investigators" had come up with, he had no answer. He had simply made it all up. Why? Because he understood that pretending that Obama was an illegitimate president soothed the racist's soul, who otherwise had to accept the idea that a Black man had won the presidency fair and square, not just once, but twice.

~ ~ ~

Trump, certainly, was not the only Republican running who was looking to pick up the white ethno-nationalist vote. This group clearly made up a sizeable percentage of the GOP electorate, and alienating them in a Republican primary was not a promising path to victory. John McCain in 2008 had famously come to Obama's defense, calling him a citizen and "a decent family man" when an attendee at one his rallies had called him an "Arab" who couldn't be trusted. Everyone had seen where McCain's honor had gotten him that November. He had the weakest enthusiasm among self-described conservatives since George H. W. Bush in his 1992 re-election campaign.

And so, pretty much every candidate did his or her best to attack Obama, even though Obama would not even be on the ballot. There was a slice of the primary voting base that was way more interested in how much you hated the Black guy than how much you hated Hillary Clinton.

This was the reason you saw Florida Senator Marco Rubio – who, remember, was considered among the more moderate ones and was supposed to be playing up the upbeat, hopeful message – offer up the theory in his stump speeches, his interviews, even the debate stage that Barack Obama did not merely have policies that Republicans disagreed with or, in the alternative, was just incompetent. Rather, Obama was actively evil, a near-treasonous villain working to weaken and damage the country he led.

"It's now abundantly clear: Barack Obama has deliberately weakened America," he told a New Hampshire audience in January 2016, repeating a theme he had been hitting the previous summer and autumn.

Of course, once the agreed-upon battleground was who could insult and vilify Barack Obama the most, Donald Trump was the hands-down champion. No one else could be as coarse and disrespectful and downright nasty. Looking at it that way, honestly, it's little wonder that he won the nomination so easily.

~ ~ ~

So is Trump himself a racist? That is, does he believe that some humans are inherently superior or inferior because of their racial or ethnic backgrounds?

For journalists, that was and remains a thorny question, for the same reason that calling Trump a liar is difficult. How do we know what's going on in his head? "Lying," after all, means knowing something is false but saying it anyway. How do we know that any given falsehood coming out of Trump's mouth at any given moment is a lie, and not the product of his vast ignorance and, possibly, dementia? Similarly on the issue of race. How do we know that any given bigoted-sounding comment of his is not simply him being an amoral jerk, pandering to his racist supporters, rather than revealing his own racism?

His critics, both outside and inside the Republican Party, scoff at the very question. Of *course* he's a racist! From the efforts to keep Black people from renting his family's apartments in the early 1970s to the ads he placed in New York

73

City newspapers in 1989 demanding the death penalty for the Central Park Five to his cheerful disparagement of Mexican immigrants in the 2016 campaign to there being "very fine people on both sides" at the neo-Nazi march on Charlottesville in 2017 to the almost recreational insults of Puerto Ricans that accompanied his attempts to block additional disaster assistance following Hurricane Maria, Trump has certainly given every appearance of being a bigot, through-and-through.

This image was solidified in the spring and summer of 2020, as Trump repeatedly professed his admiration for the "heroes" of the Confederacy, vowing to protect their statues, claiming their flag had nothing to do with slavery and even promising to veto a must-pass defense bill – one that included pay raises for all U.S. service members – because it would force military bases honoring the Confederacy to be renamed.

Yet, as always with Trump, the problem is his willingness to say whatever he believes will get him ahead at that particular instant. The Central Park Five ads, for example, were obviously trying to capitalize on the outrage of the moment, the fear that New Yorkers understandably felt after an assault like that on a random jogger. It's possible that Trump did not even consider the race of the suspects as he sought to raise his own visibility and status. Similarly, with the repeated attacks on brown-skinned immigrants, both legal and undocumented, well, Trump fully understands that that's the message his hard-core base wants to hear.

In that sense, really, it's somewhat of an academic exercise, determining whether Trump is genuinely a racist or merely behaves like one because he believes it will benefit him politically. The harm to minority communities is every bit as real either way. Hate crimes have seen a marked increase since Trump was elected. People are getting harassed, getting beaten up, even getting killed, in significantly greater numbers after Donald Trump the candidate and now Donald Trump the president seemed to signal that vilifying Black and brown people was okay again.

Perhaps that's the more important lesson to draw from Trump's behavior. That regardless of whether he himself is a racist, he is pretty certain that his voting base is racist. Proof of this, in fact, comes from his own campaign's theory of the case in the closing weeks of the 2016 election. All the major national polls had Clinton ahead by two or three points (which was, indeed, how much she won the popular vote by), but according to the Trump campaign strategists, this meant that Trump was really in the lead.

How so? Because according to their analysis, there was a "shy Trump vote" out there, constituting between three and four percent of the electorate, who were telling pollsters they were undecided, or even that they were supporting Clinton, but who would in the end vote for Trump in the privacy of the voting booth.

Why would they be ashamed of admitting they were voting for Trump? Why, indeed. Clearly it was not because of "economic anxiety" – that euphemism that far too many journalists bought into in the aftermath of the election. Voters who were worried about their jobs were quite open about that. Those I spoke to in Ohio and Pennsylvania were matter-of-factly transactional: Trump is the first candidate to come along who promises to bring back my old factory job. Not some other equally good or even better job. But the actual job I had had two or five or twenty years ago. If he doesn't deliver, I'll vote for someone else in four years.

No, what the "shy" Trump voter didn't want to admit was that he was supporting Trump because Trump had promised to keep those brown people out of our country, and to deport as many of them that are already here as possible.

Trump's pollsters and strategists understood that full well, and were counting on there being enough of them to let him sneak into the White House.

~ ~ ~

75

All that said, it is important to remember that Donald Trump did not invent this machine that feeds off of racial fear and hatred. The Republican Party did that, decades ago. Richard Nixon did not have to pander to the segregationist southern whites. He chose to do so. And so did Ronald Reagan. And so, to a lesser degree, did both Bushes. And so did countless Republican politicians at the local, state and federal levels over the last few decades.

To their credit, party leaders in 2013 tried to leave that legacy behind and move Republicans toward the inevitable future. Unfortunately for all of us, they weren't able to unload and destroy the deadly weapon they had built a half century earlier quickly enough. Donald Trump just happened to be the toddler who chanced upon it and started pulling the trigger.

5. The Stephens Find Their Stooge

In the summer and autumn of 2007, there was a guy running for the Republican presidential nomination who was saying out loud all the wink and nod stuff Republicans wanted their nativist base to believe about them without them actually having to form the words. There should be a giant wall along the southern border. All illegal immigrants in the country should be arrested and deported. Mayors of "sanctuary cities" should be prosecuted.

Sound familiar?

Eight years before Donald Trump rode down his escalator, the cheerfully open "nationalist" in the contest was a fringe congressman named Tom Tancredo. He never really had any chance of winning. Nobody outside of Colorado had ever heard of him, and even inside Colorado, he was not a statewide fixture. But his vitriol certainly had an effect on the rest of the field. Everybody else had to show how tough they would be on securing the border or risk losing support from a big slice of the primary electorate.

And even though the eventual nominee, Arizona Senator John McCain, was about as pro-immigration as a modern-day Republican can come, all the posturing caused by Tancredo wound up leaving a mark. McCain won only 31 percent of the Latino vote in November 2008, down 13 percentage points from George W. Bush's 2004 re-election campaign (which, in retrospect, will probably be the party's high-water mark for elections to come).

Two election losses later, the RNC had a plan to reverse things after 2012 nominee Mitt Romney did even worse with Latinos – 27 percent – than McCain had. The party would make an extra effort, right from the start of the new election cycle, to reach out to Latino voters and persuade them that Republicans did not hate them.

Unfortunately, nobody bothered to tell the two Stephens holed up in the tidy brick townhouse just blocks northwest of the U.S. Capitol.

~ ~ ~

As Reince Priebus and his leadership team at the Republican National Committee were plotting how to remake their party into something that could, for a change, win the popular vote in a national election by appealing to ethnic minorities, the Stephens were also plotting, in the so-called "Breitbart Embassy," home of the Washington office of the website founded by right-wing provocateur Andrew Breitbart.

Stephen Bannon was the new chief of Breitbart News after its founder died of heart failure the previous year. Bannon had been around the block more than a few times. He'd grown up in a working class family in southern Virginia, Kennedy-Catholic Democrat, until after college at Virginia Tech, when he said he lost all respect for his family's party during his years at sea in the U.S. Navy because of Jimmy Carter's leadership. Harvard Business School followed the Navy, and Goldman Sachs followed Harvard Business School. In the 1990s, he made a go of managing investments on his own in Southern California, striking it big by winding up – somewhat implausibly – with the syndication rights to the TV show *Seinfeld*. With his finances secure, Bannon turned to his real love: nativist propaganda. He started with movies, including a hagiography of former Alaska Governor Sarah Palin titled,

78

inexplicably, *The Undefeated.* Eventually, he met up with Breitbart and, after his death, took over his web site.

The other Stephen, Miller, is another beast entirely. Born well off in posh Santa Monica, Miller as a child decided to be different by being, well, kind of a jerk. In high school, to prove his superiority over the opposite sex, he once jumped in near the end of a race in a girl's track meet. Running for student government, young Stephen centered his campaign on the unfairness of asking students to pick up litter when, really, wasn't that what the custodial staff was being paid to do. Then, running for a leadership position at Boys State, Miller decided to make his campaign all about doing "black ops" and "sabotage" against the other groups.

Now there is quite naturally, and normally quite understandably, an objection that a person's high school and even college years should be off limits, that things that happened decades earlier are not accurate indicators of an adult's worldview and mindset. Except that in the case of Stephen Miller, those high school and college days are not years and years in the past, but rather, relatively recent. When Trump began his campaign in 2015, Miller was all of 29 years old. In 2013, when he and his then-boss, Alabama Senator Jeff Sessions, sabotaged a comprehensive immigration bill that had already cleared the Senate with a strong, bipartisan vote, Miller was only 27. Back then, he was known as an intemperate young man with strident, anti-immigrant views and little patience with those who disagreed with him. He would write long, angry emails to congressional reporters, with frequent deployment of the "CAPS LOCK" key, about how they were missing the important elements of the immigrant invasion and essentially acting as publicists for "open borders" Democrats.

(In April 2018, a retired neuropsychologist at Boston University's medical school wrote an essay for *Politico Magazine* lamenting Miller's nativist views and wondering what might have happened if the U.S. government had had in place the sort of anti-immigrant policies Miller favored back when his own family escaped the pogroms of Poland in the early 20th century. The author was Miller's uncle.)

In the summer of 2014, the two Stephens joined forces to figure out a way to force the 2016 Republican nominee, whoever it ended up being, to run on an anti-immigration platform. And the way to do that was to find and showcase a candidate on the Breitbart website and ancillary media ecosystem through all of 2015 to drive the whole field closer toward their views.

They succeeded beyond their wildest dreams.

~ ~ ~

The context behind this is critical to appreciate the consequences for how it all played out.

In 2014 and 2015, the Republican Party was at a crossroads. Down one path was the clearly more promising future. It required a great deal of concerted effort to broaden the base and make the party look like the country already was at that moment, but even more so where it would be in just another decade. The other path was the easier one, an even tighter embrace of the Southern Strategy that, while less effective in recent elections, had nevertheless become more appealing than ever to the primary voting base.

The party's leadership – the longtime Republican National Committee members, the major donors, the top staff – as well as the serious candidates all understood the importance of choosing Option A. Unfortunately for them, their voting base, egged on by Fox News and the associated right-wing media ecosystem, was hell bent on Option B.

The reason, of course, was the sitting president at the time, Barack Obama – not because he was a failure and did a terrible job, but because, despite everything thrown at him, he was a success, and would leave office after two terms more respected and with less scandal than any president in modern times.

Indeed, the fact he did not fail simply enraged that segment of the party that never got over the idea of a Black president, to the point where how much you hated Obama, and how vicious you were willing to be in your attacks against him, became a major, perhaps the most important, metric in the Republican primaries.

~ ~ ~

In the months and years since November 2016, one of the favorite tropes of conservatives has been that if one single person can be blamed for Trump's rise, it is Barack Obama. The 44th president, by dint of his radical policies, swung the country so far to the left and was such a divisive leader that a dramatic swing back in the opposite direction was inevitable, and Donald Trump happened to be the one carrying that message most effectively.

There is some truth in that analysis – just not in the way Trump and his apologists like to present it. Because, the fact of it is, Obama was not radical, or even particularly liberal in the policies he pursued. Those who doubt this should go talk to an actual leftist, someone who truly believes that the government should be doing far more regulating of basic business functions and breaking up big corporations and that sort of thing. To them, Obama was basically Republican-lite.

Actual progressives continue to complain that Obama should have nationalized the big banks when he had the opportunity and prosecuted the bankers and rammed through single payer health care and a path to citizenship for illegal immigrants and all those other things that a real progressive would have done without thinking twice.

The premise of their critique, of course, is correct. Obama governed far more as a centrist than what many liberals had hoped for when he ran in 2008. Taking office in the middle of the worst recession in 70 years, Obama focused on stopping it from sinking into a full-blown depression, even if that meant bringing into his administration a gaggle of Wall Street insiders whom critics argued had helped create the mess in the first place. Relatedly, he did not make prosecuting bankers who abused those risky financial products a priority for his Justice Department.

Instead, he passed a stimulus bill that in large part was tax cuts. He passed a financial reform bill that progressives argued was too weak. And to cap it all off, he passed a health care bill that was literally drafted by a conservative think tank.

And so hearing the claims from the Tea Party groups that they opposed Obama solely because of his bad policies – about the dramatic increase in the national debt in those first years of the recession; about Dodd-Frank and its handcuffing of the American financial system; about the Affordable Care Act and its imposition of socialized medicine – was puzzling. Particularly for me coming to Washington from Florida, where I had watched some of the exact same people who had busily spread nonsense about Obama being a secret Muslim born in Kenya suddenly because principled Tea Party conservatives worried sick about government spending.

The proof of what had really been going on, though, came in the first years under Trump. Here was this clearly ignorant man bullying private corporations into where they should keep or open manufacturing plants, who openly advocated breaking up tech companies whose platforms had become centers of protest against him and his policies, and whose tax cuts created annual deficits nearly as large as Obama had overseen in his first term – even though Obama was dealing with a devastating recession and Trump was enjoying the best economy in a decade. Where were the massive Tea Party protests, the guys dressed up in Revolutionary War garb and tricorn hats, demanding that Congress stand up to this massive increase in the national debt? Where was the outrage on conservative talk radio about the president's "winners and losers" as Trump ordered car makers to keep plants open in states he had won or face his wrath?

There was, of course, none of that. It turns out that the Tea Partiers really only cared about the federal debt when a Black guy was president. Mark Levin and Rush Limbaugh and Sean Hannity and the rest of them were only bothered by free-market interventions when they were being done by someone their audience hated because of the color of his skin.

Because, in the end, it really was that simple. For this sizable slice of the Republican base, opposition to Obama's policies was a fig leaf – a translucent, at best, fig leaf – for straight-up racism. The fact that Trump is doing far, far worse in the name of "America First" makes this perfectly obvious.

I personally was surprised how so many smart and reasonable people, both in politics and journalism, were unwilling to accept how big a factor racism was playing in the Tea Party movement. I recall a Washington Desk meeting at NPR in the autumn of 2011 when I pointed out how many in the Florida Tea Party crowd also happened to have been "Obama birthers" prior to his election. I was assured that, no, the Tea Party was big and diverse and primarily driven by ideology.

There was, I think, a deep resistance to accept that such open bigotry could still exist in this country. Some, clearly, was the hyper-sensitivity to accusations of "media bias" that Republicans have successfully used to delegitimize mainstream journalism for decades. But some was a genuine unwillingness to see the obvious. A sort of wishcasting that if bad behavior wasn't called out, it would sort of go away on its own.

~ ~ ~

Perhaps the reaction against Obama is best understood from the frame of reference of Americans whose primary self-identification is being white.

Yes, this is an ironic twist on conservatives who have complained for years about "identity politics," and how it was terrible that Black and Latino Democratic candidates for office would make their ethnicity a feature of their campaigns. What was almost always left unsaid was that so many white candidates were quite naturally winning a significant percentage of the white vote simply because they were white.

There was in many places all over the country but perhaps especially so in the South the understanding by a great many in the white community that Black city commissioners and state legislators and even members of Congress were unavoidable, given the imposition of single-member districts, but that statewide offices like senators and governors could safely remain in the hands of the majority. Which is to say: white people.

What Obama did by winning the presidency back in November 2008 was sucker punch an entire swath of the nation that – while cognizant that the country's demographics were changing and that they were at some point going to be in the racial minority – was completely unprepared for the idea of an actual Black president. Not in twenty years or ten or even four. But starting that January. As in not even three months away.

This was, to folks who honestly were still angry about the passage of the Civil Rights Act more than four decades earlier, a complete upending of their social order. That terrible thing that everyone knew was out there as a possibility was now suddenly upon them.

And then, when Obama won a second time in 2012, even after four years of people seeing him sitting behind that desk and flying around in that big blue airplane, this cohort of Republican voters were simply beside themselves. "Their" America was looking like it was gone, possibly never to come back.

And then, amid a field of Republican governors and senators going on and on about trade and taxes and whose experience was most relevant, was the billionaire businessman from that TV show. And he didn't care about any of that stuff. Instead, he was promising exactly what they wanted to hear: Make America Great Again – which they took to mean, Make America White Again.

As Trump would say: What the hell did they have to lose?

~ ~ ~

Of course, Donald J. Trump, it should be noted, was not the first and most obvious choice for the Breitbart Embassy's Stephens as the new, improved, more durable Tom Tancredo. He was, after all, a New Yorker who had given plenty of money to Democrats over the years – not exactly the profile of the immigrant-hating nativist they were looking for.

Indeed, Trump had demonstrated not long after Romney's loss that he was capable of the most deviant apostasy. In an interview with the right-wing *Newsmax* website (run by Mar-a-Lago member Chris Ruddy), Trump shortly after the 2012 election explained that the former Massachusetts governor had lost because he had gone off the rails on immigration. "He had a crazy policy of self-deportation which was maniacal," Trump told the publication. "It sounded as bad as it was, and he lost all of the Latino vote…. He lost the Asian vote. He lost everybody who is inspired to come into this country."

The Stephens' first choice, as it happens, was Stephen Miller's own boss, Jeff Sessions. He was certainly anti-immigrant enough, having given plenty of speeches about how the country's population included an ever-increasing percentage of people who were not born here. (In his mind, that statistic was on its face so alarming that it did not require any further explanation of its alarmingness.) But Sessions was, well, Jeff Sessions. An Alabama lawyer whose own racist comments about the NAACP had come back to bite him in his Senate confirmation hearing for a federal judgeship during the Reagan administration. The Judiciary Committee killed his nomination, with one of the "no" votes cast by Alabama's Democratic senator. It was widely understood that Sessions' desire to run for the Senate himself was at least in part to avenge that humiliation.

But Bannon was under no illusion that Sessions could possibly be the nominee. Rather, he would, as Tancredo had done, force the other candidates to speak about illegal immigration and the "browning" of America on the terms that Sessions would set, thus dragging the party closer to the Stephens' nativist ideal.

And that is the key distinction to appreciate when trying to understand Bannon and Miller's thinking, and what made them so different from typical Republican political operatives.

For the average Republican consultant, politics is like football as described by Vince Lombardi. Winning is not just the most important thing, it is the only thing. As such, policies, positions, messages and so forth are tools to be employed toward the objective: winning the election. And then the election after that. And the election after that.

For whatever it's worth, this describes neither of the Stephens. Rather, they are ideologues.

Miller, notwithstanding his quite comfortable upbringing and easy early adulthood, appears to have determined at some point that Americans of white European extraction are an endangered species, and that active steps must be taken to preserve their dominant role in the nation's culture and politics. He denies that his views amount to white nationalism – but the only real value of that assertion is to provide evidence that, even in the Trump Era, open racism is still seen as a bad thing, even to someone like Miller.

Bannon, who unlike Miller is not a child, is a more complicated study. His is clearly more of a class-based worldview, despite (or perhaps because of) his years on Wall Street. There is a cabal of transnational "elites" who have created a world economy that enriches them beyond imagination, which is screwing over ordinary working people – like, in the example he often gives, his own father, whose life savings were wiped out by the financial crisis after fifty years of working as a lineman for a major telecommunications company.

This, anyway, is his facile explanation for his unusual perspective as the leader of his "movement." Because for all of his considerable acumen and intellect, Bannon nonetheless enjoys seeing himself as a player in some epochal transformation. He buys into a deterministic historical theory that sees human progress in cycles and waves – "turning" is his preferred term of art – but in which his peculiar fetishes play a

86

key role. Cryptocurrencies, for instance, are the absolute wave of the future. And he might even convince you of this – until you remember that he once designed a business to hire low-wage Chinese computer game players to "mine" "gold" in World of Warcraft to then sell to rich gamers who didn't want to be bothered killing dragons or whatever to earn it for themselves.

In any case, Bannon's background and life experience make for a more nuanced portrait. It's quite easy to ascribe racial animus to Stephen Miller's statements and actions. Less so to Bannon – for whom the open pandering his web site did to racists and white nationalists appeared more a means to an end than necessarily a reflection of his own views.

~ ~ ~

Not that his core beliefs make much of a difference, of course, to the racial and ethnic minorities who have been the subject of vitriol at the *Breitbart* web site during the years Bannon ran it.

For those unfamiliar with the *Breitbart* brand, suffice it to say that it is not so much conservative-oriented news as it is nativist propaganda – designed to move its audience toward particular viewpoints and civic activities. Much of the printed content on Breitbart on the subjects of politics and immigration and the like was at best misleading and at worst straight-up false.

This was entirely by design. Bannon has described himself as a "Leninist" – not because he believes in a communist utopia, but because he is perfectly content with radical, disruptive societal change. As such, he is an ends-justifies-the-means kind of guy, and propaganda in service of his ideals is all good.

That approach was already evident even before the 2016 presidential race's kickoff in early 2015, in *Breitbart*'s work to kill the immigration bill, its attempts to derail the Iran nuclear agreement and its general attempts to keep its audience fired up and angry that Barack Obama was still president.

For the entire Obama second term, in fact, Breitbart News was pretty much the vanguard of right-wing hate directed at the first Black president. Article after article accused Obama of purposefully hurting the country to advance his agenda. From the 2014 influx of migrants at the southern border to the explosion of "political correctness" on college campuses to an invented epidemic of violent crime committed by illegal immigrants, Breitbart was on the case – usually in multiple takes. The overall thrust of this coverage was pretty plain: Black and brown people and their liberal elitist enablers, many of them not from the United States, were actively trying to kill, hurt or persecute ordinary Americans just trying to live their lives. And by ordinary, of course, it was understood to mean "white."

But after it became clear that Trump was – finally – serious about running for the White House himself, the Breitbart propaganda machine kicked into high gear, this time completely in service of Trump.

With his increasingly harsh language about immigrants, far harsher than any of the other candidates was willing to offer, it became evident that Trump was the Tom Tancredo of 2016 that the Stephens had been looking for, only with a much higher likelihood of blowing up the Republican establishment than the former Colorado congressman had been able to manage. After all, everyone in America knew who Donald Trump was, thanks to decades of his self-promotion through books, gossip columns and, most significant, his "reality" TV game show.

And so it was that by the time Trump came down his escalator in June 2015 and called Mexicans trying to come to this country rapists and drug dealers, there was a substantial audience ready to hear precisely that message. This was no accident, of course. Trump knew what the nativist fringe wanted to hear because Bannon was already advising him. A normal candidate would have followed up a presidential announcement with an immediate trip to Iowa or New Hampshire. Trump didn't bother with that, and instead went upstairs to give a long, in-depth interview with Bannon's

Washington bureau chief – a 28-year-old ideologue to whom Trump gave even more inflammatory remarks than he had offered in his speech.

~ ~ ~

Trump ran the laziest campaign among all the Republicans. Marco Rubio, Jeb Bush, Ted Cruz and the others had multiple events per day, spending days and weeks on end in New Hampshire and Iowa and South Carolina. They would start with breakfast meetings of local business groups and typically wouldn't finish until late at night, following a local Republican committee's chicken dinner.

Trump left Trump Tower maybe once or twice a week, right up through the final weeks of 2015. Instead, he would go down to the atrium of his building and do an appearance with a cable news show. Sometimes he wouldn't even bother going down to the camera, and would literally just phone it in from his office upstairs.

It didn't matter. His willingness to say pretty much anything for its shock value made him ratings gold for TV. And, meanwhile, Breitbart was churning out, one after the other, article after article about how great Trump and his border wall and his immigration crackdown and his trade policies would be and – maybe even more important – just how horrible Bush and Rubio and Christie would be.

It's difficult to understate the significance of this. Breitbart by 2015, having proved its muscle by tanking the immigration bill, was a must-read site in the Republican primary. Mainstream candidates understood that a lot of chatter on talk radio and a lot of the scheduling on Fox were based on the screaming, all-capitals headlines on Breitbart, and they couldn't afford to get sideways with that zeitgeist.

For his part, Bannon was not at all interested in providing a fair forum for the contenders. He is a propagandist, not a journalist. He was out to push his agenda, and he did so ruthlessly, assigning reporters to attack Bush and Rubio as much as he pumped up Trump. That treatment extended to his Sirius XM show, on which he featured Trump and massaged him through the sessions with kid gloves. Trump, as has become obvious to America now, tends to self-destruct in any type of prolonged interview, and Bannon did his best to guide the conversation and protect Trump from himself.

It was the sort of hand-holding that Trump genuinely needed at the start. He was a reality television star from New York City, not necessarily the breeding ground of right-wing conservatism. Yet with the Stephens' help, by the time voting began in early 2016, he had built enough of an advantage over enough of the field in enough of the early states that when the votes were counted the night of Super Tuesday, the party's winner-take-all rules had essentially guaranteed him the nomination.

~ ~ ~

Both Stephens eventually joined the campaign itself, first Miller, as a speech writer, and eventually Bannon. Original campaign manager Corey Lewandowski was fired in the early summer, to be replaced by longtime Republican lobbyist Paul Manafort, who in turn was fired after his financial ties to pro-Russian figures in Ukraine came out.

Bannon and pollster Kellyanne Conway – originally a Ted Cruz supporter – were brought in to salvage the foundering campaign in late summer, when it looked like Trump not only was going down, but taking the entire party with him.

How much, exactly, Bannon and Conway contributed to Trump's victory is unclear. He did, after all, get three million fewer votes overall than Clinton, and won the Electoral College by a combined margin of 77,744 votes across three states. He also had the benefit of an FBI director who wanted to teach Clinton a lesson and a Russian dictator who wanted her to lose.

The entirety of the campaign's "strategy," such as it was, was to focus on those handful of states where polling showed they had the best chance of winning – which is to say, the same as any campaign does. If there was any extraordinary achievement at all, it was in persuading Trump to read off the teleprompter and otherwise shut the hell up in that final, critical month when a big chunk of the voting pool finally tunes in to the race.

Regardless, Bannon got a ton of credit for having engineered Trump's win and went to the White House along with Miller, Conway and RNC chairman Reince Priebus. Miller became Trump's top policy adviser, Conway his ill-defined "counselor,' Priebus his chief of staff and Bannon his "chief strategist" – a campaign-like title that surprisingly wound up describing what he did, which was to try to transform as much of the Breitbart agenda that he had only been able to publish screeds about a year earlier into official United States policy.

As always, he was great at getting great press for his plans. He put up a white board in his cubby of an office listing out his agenda, and boasted of how he was marking them off as accomplished, one-by-one, before Democrats and the "Opposition Party" of the news media had a chance to figure out what was happening.

The reality, as usual, was not quite as impressive.

Yes, Trump withdrew from the Trans-Pacific Partnership and the Paris climate change accord, which impressed his base and made them believe he was getting things done. The truth of it was, though, that there was far more flash than substance. The TPP, a comprehensive trade agreement that took years to negotiate, was already hated by the Bernie Sanders wing of the Democratic Party and was likely not going to pass Congress even if Clinton had won. The Paris accord had largely been aspirational, and was going to need more work under a Clinton administration.

This is not to say there weren't negative consequences. There were, and are. The TPP agreement had been designed in large measure as a bulwark against growing Chinese influence in the region and a way to counter China's growing economic power. Our withdrawal undercut that and strengthened China. Leaving the Paris accord told the rest of the world that the United States did not take climate change seriously.

Signing executive orders and pulling out of treaty obligations is easy – but is also easily undone by the next president. And because Trump's boasts and bluster have been so over-the-top nonsensical, it has been easy for American allies to separate "Trump's" policies from "American" policies, with the expectation that the next president will do exactly that.

Further, some of that shock-and-awe campaign was so sloppily done that it hurt Trump far more in the long run than it helped – the best example being his Muslim ban.

This was the baldly bigoted pledge made in December 2015, when he vowed that as president he would simply ban Muslims from entering the country until it could be determined "what the hell is going on." It was a mean-spirited and ridiculous promise, but it was a promise, and Bannon and Miller wanted to deliver. Banning Muslims, of course, was absolutely unconstitutional, and so Miller tried to craft something that would pass muster: banning travelers from certain majority Muslim countries. He is not, however, a lawyer, and the resulting chaos was relatively quickly blocked by the courts. A watered-down version eventually was upheld, but the whole fiasco laid bare the sheer incompetence of Trump's team, right from the start.

~ ~ ~

Bannon only lasted seven months, but the nativism, xenophobia and cultivation of racists that he and Miller brought to the West Wing survive and thrive today, three and a half years later.

Again, it is important to note that the Stephens did not make Trump pander to racists. In 1989, Trump was calling for the execution of the Central Park Five, a group of Black and Latino teens, for the rape of a jogger, and continued to do so even after they had been exonerated. He rose to prominence pushing the racist lie that the country's first Black president was born in Africa. He's the one, in the end, who called Mexican immigrants rapists and drug dealers, and cheerfully vowed to ban all adherents of an entire religion from entering the country.

So, yes, they egged on his instincts rather than talking him down. Recall it was one of Bannon's final acts in the White House to advise Trump not to condemn the Charlottesville neo-Nazis and neo-Confederates, which is why he wound up claiming there were "very fine people on both sides." But they could not have made Trump do and say any of these things if Trump was not already open to them.

And, in the spring and summer of 2020, they were not the ones pushing him to make defense of the Confederacy the cornerstone of his re-election campaign, from sticking up for display of its battle flag to promising to veto a must-pass defense bill if it contained language renaming military bases that currently honor Confederate leaders.

Finally, getting Trump to sign executive orders and tweet things is not the same as making lasting changes in policy – such as, for example, by passing laws codifying those changes. On that score, neither Trump nor his Stephens was able to get any of the "Make America White Again" policies passed into law. They honestly did not even try that hard, and the one time they did – pushing Trump's hardline immigration limits during a Senate debate on a bill protecting illegal immigrants brought into the country as children – Miller's plan got just 41 votes on the floor, the fewest of any of the plans offered, with a dozen Republicans voting against it.

It was by any standard a humiliating defeat.

~ ~ ~

The biggest loser in the ascension of the Stephens in these years – apart, of course, from every American who looks or thinks differently from the typical Trump rally attendee – was the party that they hijacked to elevate their stooge. Because, in the end, neither of the Stephens really cares that much about the Republican Party and its future.

Yes, Miller worked for a Republican senator, but only because that senator was already simpatico with the anti-immigrant agenda Miller was pushing. Bannon wanted to "deconstruct the administrative state" – whatever that meant – and remake the country as "Fortress America."

Until Trump, those things were never part of the GOP worldview. Now Republicans are stuck with them, and even worse, they are stuck defending Trump's progressively more open racism.

We can accept up front that the party's record with race has not been great since the mid-1960s, as detailed earlier. Still, the reasonable people within the party, both in leadership as well as rank-and-file voters, understood full well that the coded appeals, the innuendo, the winks and nods were something to be ashamed of and were hurting the party's long-term prospects. Lee Atwater at the end of his life apologized for his enthusiastic embrace of Southern Strategy politics, while explicitly admitting that anti-welfare, anti-tax rhetoric was, in fact, a way of expressing racial animus to white voters without using objectionable words.

"You start out in 1954 by saying, 'Nigger, nigger, nigger.' By 1968 you can't say 'nigger' – that hurts you, backfires. So you say stuff like, uh, forced busing, states' rights, and all that stuff, and you're getting so abstract. Now, you're talking about cutting taxes, and all these things you're talking about are totally economic things and a byproduct of them is, Blacks get hurt worse than whites," he told Alexander Lamis, a Case Western Reserve University political scientist, in 1981.

Even Ken Mehlman, then the chairman of the Republican National Committee, in 2005 straight-up apologized at the NAACP convention for the Southern Strategy and his party's reliance on it even into the 21st Century. The party's "Growth and Opportunity Project" report after the 2012 election was largely a restatement of that acknowledgement, only this time with the admission that their tone and their message was now also hurting them with Latinos, who make up the fastest growing segment of the population.

This extended *mea culpa* from the party's intelligentsia was not anything that Trump ever bought into. Quite the opposite, in fact. From his campaign launch speech vilifying Mexicans,

Trump openly courted with a bullhorn the segment of the Republican base that Nixon originally won over with a dog whistle.

If personnel is policy, bringing the Stephens into the White House spelled out right from the start precisely the sort of administration Trump was going to have, and as the days and weeks and months passed, the policies they espoused became more and more difficult for mainstream Republicans to explain to moderate, suburban voters. College-educated, social liberals who nevertheless voted Republican because of tax policy were less than thrilled with banning entire populations from a handful of predominately Muslim countries.

In a discussion about Haitian migrants, Trump complained that they all had AIDS. About visitors from Nigeria, he warned that they would never want to return to their "huts" in Africa after they had seen the United States. Africa, by the way, was full of "shithole" countries whose residents had no business coming here in the first place.

All of this Archie Bunker-style xenophobic racism, though, paled beside what was to follow. After literal neo-Nazis marched on Charlottesville, Virginia, in a chilling torch-lit parade, complete with literal Nazi-era chants, with one of them driving into a crowd the following day, killing a counter-protester, Trump declared that there were "very fine people" on both sides. As the 2018 midterm campaign revved up, Trump began stoking anger and fear about Mexican and Central American migrants coming across the southern border, calling it an "invasion." The following summer, as a foursome of progressive minority congresswomen became more outspoken, Trump posted on Twitter that they should "go back" to the countries they had come from. (Three were born in the United States; all are citizens.) Days later, when supporters at a rally began chanting "Send her back" about one of them, Trump paused his remarks to let the chant roll for a while. A few days later, after a 21-year-old from Dallas drove to El Paso specifically to murder brown-skinned people to do his part to stop the "Hispanic invasion," Trump complained that people were unfairly blaming him.

Finally, of course, there was Trump's reaction in 2020 to the protests against the police killing of George Floyd in Minneapolis. He seemed either unwilling or unable to show even a shred of empathy, and within days reverted to form, threatening the deployment of active duty troops to cities across America and once more attacking as anti-American the NFL players who had protested police brutality by kneeling during the national anthem. He even attacked NASCAR – NASCAR! – for banning the display of Confederate flags at its events, and described "Black Lives Matter" as a hate slogan.

It has been the most stunning display of open racism in national politics in nearly five decades. George Wallace, when he ran yet again as an unreconstructed segregationist in 1972, was even then inhabiting the political fringe – not the Oval Office, seeking a second term.

Which means that if Trump winds up losing and taking the Republican Senate with him, the rising disgust among lots of moderate Republican and independent voters will be the reason why.

Meaning that the Stephens will, indeed, have changed the course of America. Just not in the direction they had hoped.

6. The Party of Lincoln Becomes the Party of Trump

In a parallel universe somewhere, within minutes of the conclusion of the first Republican debate of the 2016 election cycle in Cleveland, the one in which Donald Trump distinguished himself by saying that maybe he would support the eventual Republican nominee and maybe he wouldn't, party chairman Reince Priebus gets Trump on his cell phone with a simple, direct message: *You will get your ample posterior to DC tomorrow morning at eight, and you will sign a pledge to support our nominee next November, or you will not participate in the next debate and your bullshit candidacy in this party is over.*

Maybe Trump would have shown up and signed, maybe he wouldn't have. In either case, the power dynamics in the relationship would have been made very clear. *We* run this party, not you, and if you don't play by our rules, you're out. And given such a forceful statement from the party leadership, perhaps the other candidates would have gone after Trump hard and early, when opinions were still malleable. In this alternate timeline, Trump's numbers would have succumbed to gravity as enough GOP voters learned of his various frauds and scams with months to go before voting began, rather than just days and weeks.

Of course, in the universe *we* inhabit, that's not what happened at all.

Instead, Priebus some days later went to Trump's home in New York, and up on the "26th" floor which in reality is the 18th floor but which for marketing purposes is mis-numbered, Priebus asked Trump very nicely and politely if he wouldn't mind signing this pledge to support the party's eventual nominee. Trump did so, with his great big, bold, up-and-down cursive he so loves to show off – and then not long afterward said that he would honor his promise ... so long as the party wasn't mean to him.

In one of the classic essays of the 2016 election, Florida Republican political consultant Rick Wilson likened Priebus to a frightened hobbit scurrying to Trump's Barad-dûr and in the process signing away the party's ability to manage Trump in any meaningful way. Trump is profoundly ignorant of just about every topic necessary to effectively govern a small town, let alone a major nation, but he does possess the attributes of a schoolyard bully – one of which is to sense fear and exploit it.

Trump could see where things stood. The Republican Party was afraid of him. He may not have understood why, but that did not matter. He could do as he pleased, and they would not say boo.

Of course, their reasons for fearing Trump were entirely misplaced. In the autumn of 2015, I was told that the concern was that if the party leaders angered Trump, he would run as an independent and draw off votes from their nominee, much as Ross Perot had done in 1992 from President George H.W. Bush. That baffled me at the time, and continues not to make any sense. Ross Perot spent $64 million of his own fortune in that 1992 race. That's $108 million in 2016 dollars.

The Republican National Committee had a well-financed and competently staffed research unit that all day, every day, cranked out one piece of opposition research after another about Hillary Clinton. Could no one on that staff be spared for even 10 minutes to Google around a little bit to get up to speed on Donald Trump? Maybe "discover" that he was a fabulist extraordinaire, a serial bankruptor of *casinos*, the subject of thousands of lawsuits accusing him of failing to honor his contracts and, most germane to their fears, not nearly as rich as he liked to claim?

I was told by the RNC, in early 2016, after Trump had essentially locked up the nomination after winning New Hampshire, South Carolina, Nevada and Florida: No, that wasn't the party's job.

As Trumpism runs its inevitable course and the Republican Party's obituary is written, the final cause of death will be seen as having taken hold, untreated, in those months of summer and autumn, 2015: A deadly blend of incompetence and cowardice.

~ ~ ~

It is certainly true that the Republican Party establishment did not want Donald Trump when he entered the race. In that first debate in Cleveland, when he started insulting the other candidates, accusing them all of being on the take, they booed him heartily, and they meant it.

They understood what a long-term threat he was to the party, that he was undoing all the work they had put in to make the GOP viable a decade down the road. They understood that he was essentially a carnival barker, saying incendiary things because he craved attention, not because he had any coherent platform. They assumed he would not only lose, but that he would get utterly annihilated by Hillary Clinton, making them lose the Senate and perhaps come dangerously close to losing the House.

That, right there, is the key to understanding what followed.

To most party leaders who opposed Trump in the summer and autumn of 2015, it wasn't so much that they were appalled by his overtly racist, often misogynistic appeals. It was that they feared those appeals would lead to a historic loss.

And so, when Trump despite everything managed to win, there was an almost immediate recalibration of thinking. Perhaps the 2013 "autopsy" had gotten it all wrong. Perhaps the path to success in the coming decades was the one Trump had followed. Rather than purge the racist talk, ramp it all the way up instead, and mix in some protectionist, fortress America stuff to win back the industrial Midwest.

As one top RNC member, someone integrally involved with Republican presidential campaigns going back to George H.W. Bush's runs answered me when I asked about the implications for the party's moral and philosophical underpinnings: "We won. That's what we're supposed to do."

~ ~ ~

If the party intelligentsia was operating under the – flawed – assumption that Trump would mount an independent White House run if he felt slighted by the Republican Party, the candidates themselves were working under a completely different assumption: That Trump was such an absurd cartoon that real Republican primary voters would never take him seriously. That he was riding high in the early polls for the same reason that Herman Cain and Michelle Bachmann briefly led GOP polls in the 2012 race. He was unusual and entertaining – but that once the real electorate started paying attention, he would quickly fade. Or, given Trump's predilection for saying preposterous things, he would eventually go too far, explode and then collapse, leaving the primary field to the grownups.

This was because the serious candidates who could afford even the most modest staffs *had* spent their ten minutes of due diligence on Google and knew perfectly well what a fraud and a liar Trump had proven himself to be over the decades. His was such an over-the-top con, in fact, that the candidates for the most part couldn't be bothered to waste their time knocking him down. What would be the point? He would be gone soon enough anyway.

In the autumn of 2015, the major campaigns all had strategies about how to win or place in enough early contests to make it to Super Tuesday and hope for a big night there. None of those strategies involved worrying about Donald Trump. That, in retrospect, was the only reason Trump was able to win the nomination. It's important to remember that even by midspring 2016, with most of the original cast of 17 candidates having already dropped out, Trump still had only received about a third of all the primary ballots cast. He clearly was not the runaway favorite.

But with the other candidates not only sniping at one another on the stump but spending millions of dollars in attack ads against each other, Trump was left relatively unscathed heading into the first contests. There has come to be a mythology about this in the years that have passed, that somehow Trump was immune to attacks from the others, and in fact grew even stronger when the "establishment" tried to take him down.

This is nonsense, and there was clear evidence that it was nonsense available in real time. In October, 2015, the conservative Club for Growth spent $1 million on a limited run of ads in Iowa attacking Donald Trump. And, in that same time period, Trump's support in Iowa appreciably dropped, from 28 points down to 20 points, within a couple of weeks. The group in fact publicized this with the message: Trump can be stopped in the traditional way, and we have shown it's possible, but we're not interested in doing it by ourselves so the rest of you need to step up. Alas, no one else stepped up, and Trump's numbers rose back to where they had been soon after the Club's attack ads stopped running.

If there was any one candidate who had the means to go on the air and destroy Trump, it was Jeb Bush. The former Florida governor had been able to amass more than $100 million in a superPAC controlled by his longtime campaign strategist. If the Club for Growth had shown that Trump was vulnerable in the traditional way, with television ads pointing out his many hypocrisies to the Republican voting base, it was Bush who had at his disposal the means to finish the job. A couple of months of those ads ramped up to saturate the market – not that costly, in Iowa; TV rates are cheap – and Trump's number might have been driven down into the low teens or even single digits, and that would have been it for him.

But Jeb Bush did not take out Donald Trump. Instead, he went after fellow Floridian Marco Rubio with a vengeance.

Having covered both men during the years of Bush's tenure in Tallahassee, I can understand what that was about. Rubio had risen to the cusp of becoming speaker of the Florida House during Bush's two terms, not because of his command of policy, but because he was a good networker and a great orator. He was, compared to Bush, an ignoramus on substantive matters, and, frankly, never that terribly interested in working to change that. That he would nonetheless jump into a presidential race against Bush was something that would have driven Jeb crazy – and it became clear that if Bush was not going to be the nominee, he would make sure that Rubio wouldn't either.

~ ~ ~

In fairness to Bush, he was not the only candidate who failed to take on Trump in any serious fashion until it was too late. None of the others did, either.

Some of them were just plain afraid that he would ridicule them with some childish taunt that his fan base would find uproarious, as he had done to Bush by calling him "low energy." Others calculated that, eventually, they would need to woo Trump's supporters after he dropped out, and that attacks on Trump would make doing so more difficult, if not impossible, when that time came.

Rick Tyler, a top aide in the Ted Cruz campaign, told me that their polling and focus groups had led them to believe that Trump's relationship with his followers was more akin to a pop star's hold on his fans than that of a typical politician's appeal to his supporters. Attacking or insulting Trump, the Cruz camp felt, would not weaken Trump at all, just make it impossible for Cruz to pick up Trump's fans, who would migrate to candidates who had not attacked Trump, or just drop out of the voting pool entirely.

Cruz's strategy to take advantage of that: become a Trump fan himself. Agree with him on the debate stage. Mention him in speeches. Praise him at every opportunity. Make himself the most obsequious Trump-wanna-be that could exist, all with the idea that when inevitably Trump left the race, his people would turn to Cruz as the next best thing.

Of course, this plan lacked any sort of contingency for the scenario that wound up happening, which was Trump staying atop the polls – in no small measure because none of the others were attacking him – and thereby making the "maximum suck-up" strategy somewhat counterproductive. After all, how could anyone take Cruz seriously when he suddenly turned on Trump in early 2016 after listening to him for months say how wonderful and smart Trump was?

So it was with the other two left in the race toward the end. When Rubio began trying to insult Trump at his own, sophomoric level, the resulting incongruity was laughable. Rubio for months avoided speaking ill of Trump, but now was taunting him for having a small penis? John Kasich, similarly, spent so little time criticizing Trump's tone and his blatantly racist appeals during the first nine months of the campaign that it obviously raised the question of why he was only bringing them up so late, with Trump holding a commanding lead.

~ ~ ~

In truth, Trump did have a loyal following, but the singular reason for this, as discussed earlier, was his willingness to say those things about immigrants and minorities – all of those "others" who are endangering the *real* America – that the Republican Party and its presidential nominees had only been willing to wink at in past years. Why go with a maybe, sort-of racist sympathizer when you could vote for the real deal?

That percentage of the Republican base driven primarily by racial animus and anxiety had no reason to go elsewhere. Yet that group alone was not enough to have given Trump anywhere close to a majority of the votes cast in the primaries. In other words, he could have been beaten, had the rest of the Republican field, or the party apparatus itself, made it their first-order mission to do so.

They did not. In the case of the party leadership, they never even tried.

Perhaps the most amazing spectacle as the primaries closed out was witnessing the emergence of a die-hard group of Republican activists who started plotting a revolt at the coming summer convention in Cleveland to deny Trump the nomination … and watching the party establishment squash them like a bug. Some were foreign policy conservatives, who saw in Trump an alarming fondness for Russian dictator Vladimir Putin. Some were budget hawks, who worried (correctly, as it turned out) that Trump had no interest in limiting spending, and would quickly run up huge deficits. Many, perhaps most, were genuinely religious Christians who could not for the life of them understand how their party could be on the brink of nominating someone as shamelessly immoral as Donald Trump. It wasn't just the serial divorces and the repeated affairs. It was his willingness to lie and cheat about everything in his life, and then to brag about it.

This was, of course, not the larger universe of self-described evangelical Christians, who happily fell in with Trump and whom we'll explore more fully in the next chapter.

These anti-Trump activists, particularly the religious conservatives, wanted no part of Donald Trump, and led the charge in the pre-convention Rules Committee to permit delegates to follow their "conscience," if they found they truly could not support him.

If ever there was a presumptive nominee with a nonexistent grasp of party rules and potential machinations, it was Donald J. Trump. The party leaders could easily have gone along with the activists' demands and manipulated the rules to allow for a floor challenge, and a floor challenge – again, recall that Trump had not won a majority of the votes cast and was relying on delegates who disliked him to vote for him – might well have succeeded.

Recall also, at the time, that the smart people in the party were convinced that Trump would not only lose, but lose by huge margins. (They could not have known then that Putin would be throwing his considerable weight behind Trump or that James Comey would also insert himself into the race in the final days, unintentionally but decidedly on the side of Trump.)

The "Never Trumpers," as they had started to call themselves, made that a top selling point in their sales pitch to fellow delegates: For the sake of every other Republican running all over the country, Trump had to be removed, and here was the way to do it.

Their entreaties, though, did not find many receptive ears, at least among the party leaders who had the power to make things like that happen. Leadership's logic was simple and, to be fair, understandable. The party may not have liked that Donald Trump had won the nomination, but he had, through legitimate Republican voters casting legitimate ballots. Not a majority, no, but with a large enough margin over the next highest vote getter that wresting the nomination from him would be worse than letting him stay and getting pummeled in November.

~ ~ ~

Through all of this post-game analysis, that is an important thing to remember. Republican leaders in the summer of 2016 believed they were in a no-win situation. Donald Trump was their nominee, and because of that they faced the real threat of losing the Senate in addition to watching Democrats extend their hold on the White House to at least twelve years. Yet if they pulled strings to let the Never Trumpers take it away from him, they risked watching some percentage of Trump's primary voters – half? two-thirds? – refuse to vote for Republicans up and down the ticket that fall. They would definitely lose the Senate, they believed, and probably the House as well.

And so they shut down the dissent. The Never Trumpers' best chance was in the Rules Committee, and the party establishment made sure to strong-arm enough votes to kill any rules changes right there. When the faction made a final try on the floor, that, too, was quickly dispensed with.

The fact there was a rebellion at all, of course, became an element in the building conventional wisdom that Trump was headed for a wipeout. Utah Senator Mike Lee, a respected conservative but still considered part of the Republican establishment, delivered a noteworthy speech in the Rules Committee, pleading with Trump's people. "This angst isn't going to go away just because we papered over it with rules," Lee said. "I say to Mr. Trump, and those aligned with him, make the case to those delegates who want to have a voice."

And Texas Senator Ted Cruz, who had stayed in the running against Trump until the Indiana primary in early May, delivered a speech from the stage that finished without ever endorsing Trump and instead told the delegates to vote their conscience. He was booed off the stage by the front-and-center New York State delegation, but cheered by a notable percentage of both the floor and the audience.

The roll call of the states produced another awkward moment, with lackluster applause as Trump's home state gave him the delegates necessary to secure the nomination and Frank Sinatra's "New York, New York" filled the arena. While pro-Trump New York, Pennsylvania and California delegates at the front cheered and swayed to John Kander and Fred Ebb's Big Apple anthem, entire state delegations at the sides and back of the floor remained seated.

Further, it was not just the ideologically motivated activists who were unhappy with their new nominee. The party's professionals, those who do the grunt work of turning candidacies into election victories, were similarly dreading what was to come next.

Indeed, while much air time and ink and pixels have been spent discussing how bad a candidate Clinton was, comparatively little has been spent on the inverse: analyzing just how terrible a candidate Trump proved himself to be that autumn. He could not stay on "message." He constantly invented absurd controversies for himself. His refusal to sleep anywhere but his own bed in Trump Tower each night drastically curtailed his campaign schedule. And he felt next to no responsibility in helping down-ballot candidates.

There is a reason the seasoned hands at the Republican Party had had nightmares over the prospect of a Donald Trump nomination. Never mind the terrible long-term consequences for the party's attempts to build bridges with the emerging America. Never mind how badly he was polling with women, who, it might be helpful to remember, make up a majority of the country. Just from a basic, blocking-and-tackling standpoint, they knew full well that Trump's "campaign" was but a Potemkin village, with minimal staff, no finance structure to raise money, no network of volunteers to turn out the vote. It was basically Trump, selling hats to pay for the jet fuel that let him fly around the country holding rallies that fed his ego, and taking advantage of the free TV time the cable networks were giving him because, well, there are 24 hours in each day that need to filled with programming, and Trump was good for ratings.

The party professionals knew that if somehow Trump was the nominee, there would be no "merger" of staffs and operations, as in previous campaigns. The Republican National Committee would basically have to carry Trump on their backs, doing all the basics that have to happen in a campaign but for which Trump had exactly zero concern.

And not long after the convention was over, party officials got quick confirmation that they had been correct to worry. With neither the ability nor much of an interest in raising money for the general election, Trump was instead demanding that the Republican National Committee reallocate $150 million originally designated for congressional races and state parties to his presidential run.

Longtime RNC leaders were incensed. One of Trump's purported great advantages over the other candidates was that he had so many extra billions of dollars laying around that he wouldn't need to ask any special interests for money, and would instead be able to spend whatever he needed out of his own pocket. At one point, he had said he would even be willing to spend $1 billion of his own money to win. Yet now that he had the nomination, he was telling the party that he wanted $150 million of *their* money?

Republicans understood, though, that they had no choice. Trump now had them over a barrel. He had no knowledge of the mechanics of turning out voters. When I staked out his Iowa headquarters for a day leading into the caucuses, there had been virtually no activity there at all, in contrast to all of the other serious candidates who had streams of staffers and volunteers in and out as they reached out to actual voters. Trump intended to continue the strategy that had won him the nomination: flying around the country holding rallies, with his costs covered by the his fans buying his "MAKE AMERICA GREAT AGAIN" hats.

RNC members and staff realized that while that sort of campaign would stroke Trump's massive ego – letting him do pretty much the only part of running for president that he enjoyed – it would do virtually nothing for the down-ticket candidates who needed Trump to drive turnout for any chance of winning themselves. If they didn't give his campaign the money he demanded, he would lose by an even bigger margin and pretty much guarantee that Republicans would lose Congress, as well. They gave him the money.

"It was the biggest waste of $150 million I'd seen in my life," a top RNC official told me privately.

~ ~ ~

The personal views of many of their leaders toward their new nominee notwithstanding, the RNC itself was in decent shape in the summer of 2016. The party and its 2012 nominee Mitt Romney had been outmatched by Democrats and Barack Obama's campaign on the nuts-and-bolts, data-driven voter turnout operation four years earlier, but they had made up a lot of lost ground in the intervening years.

They were also helped by the schism created in the Democratic Party by challenger Bernie Sanders, whose attacks on Hillary Clinton and the entire "system" had never fully healed and whose efforts to help Clinton in the autumn campaign were half-hearted, at best. Sanders, for example, refused to turn over his e-mail list to the Democratic National Committee, hampering the Clinton campaign's efforts to win over Sanders' primary voters.

But even leaving aside the Democrats' problems, the Republicans had, in fact, followed through on some of the technical recommendations in their "autopsy" from three years earlier. Yes, Trump had torched the portions having to do with reaching out to minorities to expand the party's base, but they had indeed put RNC staff on the ground in key states to essentially create a turnkey voter mobilization operation for whichever candidate won their nomination. In 2013 they had expected that candidate to be Jeb Bush or Marco Rubio or Ted Cruz, true, but the existence of that organization wound up being critical, because Trump had nothing of the sort.

In other words, even though they thought Trump would get crushed come November and that his inability and unwillingness to raise money could mean a wipeout in the Senate and the House as well, they were pros, and did their jobs anyway.

Late that summer and into early autumn, it did not look particularly hopeful at all. Trump was down double digits, and it looked like there was a good chance President Hillary Clinton would have a Democratic-run Senate and pick up some seats in the House, too.

But then, by mid-autumn, the race began to tighten. With Trump's explicit promise to appoint federal judges pre-approved by the right-wing Federalist Society, Republicans who had opposed Trump in the primaries and had previously said they would sit the election out started coming around – led, amazingly enough, by self-described evangelical Christians.

That phenomenon is particularly illustrative of the Christian Right's evolution, and will be explored in greater detail later.

But for now, by October, it began to appear that Trump might truly have a chance, if he was able to flip a few states in the Midwest that Democrats had perennially won in addition to

Obama states Ohio and Iowa, where Trump already appeared likely to win. Few longtime RNC regulars believed he would actually pull it off. More than one previous Republican nominee had believed they would win Pennsylvania or Wisconsin, only to wind up a solid seven or eight points back come election night. But what the tighter race did mean was a better chance of holding onto the Senate, giving Republicans the opportunity of stifling Clinton's agenda from day one. Indeed, some Republican senators even started talking about blocking her from filling the open Supreme Court seat that Majority Leader Mitch McConnell had already prevented Obama from filling.

~ ~ ~

The October 7 publication of the "Access Hollywood" tape at first seemed like it would change everything.

After all, more than half of the electorate is female. What had been a pretty sure thing for Hillary Clinton suddenly became a 100-percent can't miss lock. Reince Priebus, whose timidity had allowed Trump to remain a viable Republican candidate more than a year earlier, begged Trump to drop out, explaining that he couldn't possibly win and would bring ruin on the Republican Party and all of its other candidates.

That was, naturally, exactly the wrong argument to make with Trump. What did he possibly care about the Republican Party? What did that organization have to do with him? If Priebus had been thinking clearly, he would have told him that remaining in the race would destroy his "brand" forever, and that if he wanted to remain a billionaire, he needed to drop out. For his own sake, for his kids' sake.

On the other side was Stephen Bannon, who, when asked, told Trump to remain in the race and guaranteed "100 percent" that Trump would win. That was nonsense bluster, of course, but it was nonsense bluster that Trump wanted to hear.

Not at all coincidentally, as now proven by the August 2020 release of the Senate Intelligence Committee report on the 2016 election, within minutes of the Access Hollywood tape's release, WikiLeaks began posting emails stolen from Clinton campaign chairman John Podesta by Russian spies. Suddenly there was a competing story to Trump's "grab 'em by the pussy" boast – and, amazingly enough, despite not knowing the emails' provenance, media outlets began publishing them.

Within a few days, the polling had stabilized. Within another week, with daily releases of more stolen emails and with Trump now urging his rally and his television audiences to read that Russian material for themselves, and wasn't it great that WikiLeaks was doing this fantastic public service, Trump had nearly returned to where he had been before the publication of the tape.

The party was back in business.

~ ~ ~

True, through those final weeks, they still expected to lose, but things were looking better for holding onto both chambers of Congress, which was what they were really focused on, anyway.

Trump, his supporters and, ensconced now in Trump Tower, the RNC staff essentially doing the grunt work of a presidential candidate's campaign, began centering their efforts around the WikiLeaks material being dribbled out on a near-daily basis. Most of it was nonsense – a pair of top staffers, both Catholic, discussing the Church's ongoing issues; Podesta's risotto recipe – but a few things were genuinely damaging to Clinton. The text of her speech to bankers, for example, in which she did not berate them for their greed and threaten to throw them in jail, which is what many Bernie Sanders supporters wanted to hear. It wasn't really the content of the emails, but the fact they were being released daily, that so many news outlets were eagerly reporting on them, that Trump was talking about them as exposing Clinton's "corruption" every single night in his rallies – the ongoing drip made it seem to uncritical observers that an enormous scandal was unfolding.

In truth, of course, an enormous scandal *was* unfolding, right out in the open.

Trump and his campaign had already been told, back in August, that those emails had been stolen by the Russians, who had given them to WikiLeaks to release. In fact, also on Oct. 7, an hour before the Access Hollywood tape was published, the Office of the Director of National Intelligence and the Department of Homeland Security had put out a statement explicitly connecting the computer hacks to the Russians, and even naming WikiLeaks as a Russian ally.

That Trump and most of his commandeered party went ahead and used it anyway had enormous implications for the coming years. Once upon a time, the Republicans had been the party of national security, of "America First" in the sense that political disagreements should end at the nation's borders. Of standing up for the intelligence community as critical for the country's safety in a dangerous world. Donald Trump, with his open embrace of Russia's dictator and his continual disparagement of the United States national security services, took a blow torch to all of that, and Republicans stood by silently or, even more amazing, joined right in.

In fairness, not every Republican was willing to do this. Florida Senator Marco Rubio, running for re-election, refused to use the WikiLeaks material, explaining that the Russians were helping his party that year, but would be helping Democrats the next time around or the time after that, and that in any event no candidate should accept foreign help.

He was, though, a rare exception. Far too many Republicans pretended as if the emails were a magical gift from heaven, rather than private material stolen by a foreign government for the specific purpose of helping their preferred candidate in the American presidential election – even though our own intelligence agencies had already come out and said so.

~ ~ ~

112

Republicans got another boost in the campaign's final days, when FBI Director James Comey, apparently pressured by agents from the New York City field office, wrote a letter to Congress explaining that he was reopening the investigation into Clinton's use of a private email server for her government business. Investigators had found new emails on the laptop of disgraced former congressman Anthony Weiner, the husband of a top Clinton aide. Barely a week later, he wrote a second letter, saying the review of those emails had found nothing new, and the case was, again, closed.

And within a few days, it became clear that that had been the final factor – that last crossways wave train from yet another direction – that added just enough height to that Trump rogue wave to let him squeak out wins in Wisconsin, Michigan and Pennsylvania and take the presidency. Exit polling showed that voters who decided in the final week broke 49 to 41 in Trump's favor, and it's easy to understand why. For those who genuinely thought Trump was potentially dangerous but didn't trust Clinton, the fact of a renewed investigation suggested that maybe she really was corrupt like everyone had been saying, and that Trump was the lesser of two evils. And for irregular voters who were leaning toward Trump but not terribly likely to vote, the second letter may well have been the proof that the system truly was rigged, just as Trump had been screaming about, and served as the impetus to get them to actually turn out.

In the closing days, though, national polling numbers had settled back close to where they had been pre-Comey-letters, and Republicans were again largely preparing to lose the White House and possibly the Senate. Never-Trumpers and Hold-Your-Nose-Trumpers, both, were thinking of how to take back control of their party. The radical reforms that would be necessary, the painful divorce from that portion of the "base" that had given Trump the nomination.

At the RNC, top leaders were also making plans for after the loss. Priebus would stay on through the winter meeting, but then would step down. And at the campaign itself, top staffers were busy making calls trying to smooth things over with the non-Trump Republican world to make re-integration possible.

Trump, meanwhile, had kept adding rallies to the election eve schedule, as if trying to squeeze every last ounce of self-affirmation he could from his adventure. In Manchester, New Hampshire, as he left the stage, he lingered for long moments, looking wistfully at the Southern New Hampshire University hockey arena crowd, knowing that after that night, that part of his life would be behind him for good.

Back before he became a Trump apologist and defender, Ari Fleischer was one of his harshest Republican critics in the summer and fall of 2015.

A former press secretary to President George W. Bush and an author of the 2013 GOP autopsy that made outreach to Latinos a top priority, Fleischer warned that Trump, unless he was stopped, would radically change the Republican Party, for the worse and forever. Since the time of Ronald Reagan, the party had relied on a "three-legged stool" of fiscal, national security and social conservatives. Trump had zero in the way of an underlying political philosophy, unless self-aggrandizement and endless lying can be considered one.

"It certainly won't resemble the stool anymore," he told me in March of 2016, as we discussed a Donald Trump-led Republican Party. "It's bizarre because it has no principled coherent ideology that we're used to."

All of that changed, almost instantaneously and without warning, close to midnight on November 8, 2016.

Again, Trump and his campaign were so prepared for a quick and decisive loss that they had rented a space more fitting for a county party convention than a presidential election night. The Hilton Midtown ballroom was decidedly cramped, with room for perhaps a few hundred between the stage and the television risers. It was chosen because Trump Tower and the candidate's penthouse condo were only four blocks away. Trump could breeze in at around 10, after some key states were called for Clinton, give a short speech and then go the hell home.

Trump started the trip there in the middle of the evening, showing up at his campaign "war room" fifty floors below his Trump Tower penthouse – only to learn that he had won North Carolina and was winning Florida and Ohio and Iowa and could well win Michigan and Pennsylvania. The prospect of actually becoming president so unnerved him that he scurried back up to his residence to collect himself.

No less stunned was the Republican Party establishment, which had assumed it would need to conduct yet another "autopsy" and issue yet another report, or possibly the same report, with some minor updates, as it had four years earlier.

Trump gave a gracious speech that night and for a few weeks after that seemed as if he might govern like a normal, rational human being. His visit to the *New York Times* editorial board two weeks after his election, for example, was perhaps his all-time high point, by way of normalcy.

All of that, of course, came to a crashing end soon enough. The FBI had six months earlier opened a counterintelligence investigation into Trump's campaign, and the outgoing Obama administration made sure to make public as much as it could about the assistance Trump had received from Russia to become president. This, predictably, enraged Trump and he responded, also predictably, by picking a fight that continues to this day with federal intelligence officers and prosecutors. Meanwhile, behind the scenes, the Trump transition was busy jettisoning all the work that Chris Christie had done to prepare for a possible Trump victory. Trump had never even liked the idea of having a transition team in the first place, after he learned that either he or his campaign, under federal law, would have to pay their salaries. After the election, Christie was unceremoniously dumped, publicly replaced by Vice President-Elect Mike Pence, privately replaced by son-in-law Jared Kushner and in reality replaced by ... nobody.

This was possibly the most underappreciated development of the Trump first term. Late in the campaign, when I pushed senior Republicans at the RNC on how they were going to deal with the possibility of Trump actually winning, I was assured that should that eventuality somehow come to pass, that Governor Christie had it under control. Trump himself had neither the capacity nor any interest in governing, true, but the federal bureaucracy was big and unwieldy and the people Christie was lining up were competent professionals who would know how to manage it and keep the country running just fine, notwithstanding the occupant of the Oval Office.

When all those competent pros with experience in previous Republican administrations – most of whom had in some form or fashion criticized Trump over the previous eighteen months and were, therefore, unacceptably disloyal – were removed from the talent pool, what was left? Turns out, very little.

Lots of lower-level political appointee jobs went unfilled for months. Some still remain unfilled. Others went to young men and women whose sole qualification had been working in some capacity for Trump's election. A disproportionate number wound up getting fired after news reports detailed social media histories full of racism and white nationalism.

A "senior administration official" during a briefing with reporters in early 2019 blamed Trump's inability to get a handle on illegal immigration – recall, he had promised his core supporters that he alone among the Republicans running would be able to end the problem – on the inability to find Trump supporters who were also competent managers. "The skill set that translates to managing a large and sometimes very recalcitrant bureaucracy is a very different skill set, sometimes, from working at a think tank or drafting messaging amendments or doing blogging," he said in the days following a housecleaning of insufficiently Trumpist top staff at the Department of Homeland Security.

~ ~ ~

Trump and his aides' behavior and language in office has been at times nothing short of appalling. Trump repeatedly uses "official" speeches to attack political opponents and boost allies. He disparages judges and journalists who challenge him.

Many of his political appointees have mimicked this, repeatedly putting themselves at odds with the Hatch Act that prohibits political activity on government property and government time (Trump is exempt).

Yet all of that can be reversed in the next administration, whether that's Joe Biden next year or Mike Pence or some other Republican or Democrat in five. There are laws, after all, governing executive branch conduct, and at some point they will be enforced again.

The changes Trump has wrought to the Republican Party are another matter entirely.

As Ari Fleischer predicted, Trump has smashed Reagan's three-legged stool and it seems doubtful it can ever be put back together. By appearing subservient to the Russian dictator who put him into office, even ignoring intelligence reports that Russia had offered a $100,000 bounty for each American soldier killed in Afghanistan, he has ended Republicans' claim to be the party of national security. By pushing a $2 trillion tax cut while simultaneously jacking up spending, he has demolished the fiction that it's the party of fiscal sanity. And by being, well, Donald Trump – appearing to lack even the slightest interest in common decency – he has exposed the loudest voices in the Christian political community who unabashedly continue to support him for what they really are.

Finally, and to most voters most importantly, his initial indifference, then cartoonish ineptitude, then indifference again about the pandemic that continues to ravage our country makes it impossible for Republicans to run as the party of competence.

Republicans who truly cared about a rational foreign policy or balancing the federal budget or wanting elected leaders to live by a moral framework to a large degree have stopped thinking of themselves as Republicans. At the city, county and state levels, this has meant that local Republican parties have begun to sound and act more like Donald Trump, following the lead of the RNC in shrugging and accepting Trumpism as the new normal.

One former high-ranking RNC member told me privately that the mid- and long-term consequences of having Trump in the White House and as the standard bearer for their party had not really sunk in for activists who see things more through the frame of winning and losing. Their side had won. That's the only thing that was important. It was their turn to get the fancy sounding job titles in Washington and the ambassadorships and the board appointments from which they had been shut out for eight years.

"It's like kids in a candy story," he told me.

It truly was astonishing. Literally the same adult human beings at the Republican National Committee who less than two years earlier had rolled their eyes and shaken their heads at Donald Trump's silly insults and childish nicknames took to describing them as "branding" genius, as proof of Trump's brilliance.

At the 2019 winter RNC meeting in Albuquerque, New Mexico, Jeff Kent, a longtime committeeman from Washington state, known as a fairly establishment figure, put forward a resolution to support Donald Trump's re-election, making it clear that the party was going to put its collective thumb on the scales against any potential challenger. "To the press in the back of the room," Kent said, pointing to us reporters, "please go tell the world we will always proudly wear this hat and we will always proudly support our great president, Donald J. Trump." Then he donned a red "MAKE AMERICA GREAT AGAIN" ball cap to cheers. The resolution passed unanimously.

At state and local levels, Republicans who criticized Trump were run out of their committees and clubs. Sometimes they were defeated in elections, and sometimes it was simply made clear to them that their views were no longer welcome.

Kendal Unruh had been a Republican activist for decades and considered herself a front-line soldier in the battle to save America from liberals. She had attended eight Republican conventions heading into 2016, and when Trump started gathering steam in the GOP primaries, she fought his candidacy as hard as she could. When he won the nomination anyway, she became one of the leaders in the effort to dump him at the summer convention in Cleveland. And then, when that failed and Trump won the presidency, the 55-year-old teacher at a Christian school in suburban Denver found that her local Republican committee no longer had any use for her.

"It's not the party that I knew, but it's the party they have become. They will violate their own moral consciences to unequivocally support him. They have lost the high road. They had it, and they lost it. I hope it was worth selling their souls," she told me two years later. "It's not the Republican Party anymore. It's the Trump Party."

It was just as well that she left of her own accord. Donald Trump's Republican Party has little room for dissent, and no room at all for criticism of the dearest leader. Even after he had been impeached for extorting Ukraine into helping his re-election by smearing the Democrat he feared most as a challenger, and it was within Senate Majority Leader Mitch McConnell's power to rid his party and the nation of Donald Trump once and for all, he would not do it.

It truly is a wonder they haven't gone ahead and just renamed the party after him.

7. God, Guns and Russia

One early June afternoon in 2011, Barack Obama walked off the golf course, into his presidential limo, and then into a nearby church where he strode onto the stage. He had thrown a blazer over his sweaty golf duds but was still wearing his golf cleats as he was prayed over by the pastor and the congregation. He didn't even bother taking off his hat when he first entered the sanctuary.

Obama, of course, never did any such thing.

But it's fun to imagine what the reaction would have been if he had. Christian conservatives would have been calling for his head, outraged to the point of triggering strokes, for the utter lack of respect he had shown for their faith, let alone common decency, and how *dare* he! Fox News and Rush Limbaugh and the rest of the right-wing fog machine would have been in high dudgeon for weeks, at the least. Republican members of Congress would have queued up to register their outrage to the C-SPAN cameras. Some might have even decided that this time the secret Kenyan Muslim had gone too far, and that his behavior constituted a "high crime and misdemeanor" and, more in sorrow than in anger, introduced articles of impeachment.

Contrast all of that to how those groups responded when this precise thing actually did occur on June 2, 2019, and you have a perfect window into the perverse relationship between Donald J. Trump and the American evangelical community of the early 21st century.

~ ~ ~

At 1 p.m. on that afternoon, David Platt had just finished up his sermon at McLean Bible Church in the Tyson's Corner neighborhood of suburban Fairfax County, Virginia, when he was notified that the White House wanted him to pray for President Trump, who was, in fact, pretty much on his way over there.

Platt did what pretty much any pastor would do in that situation. He told the White House, yes, the president was welcome, and that he would indeed pray for him. Just over an hour later, Platt brought onto the stage a sweaty, disheveled, still wearing his khakis and golf shirt under a blazer, still wearing his golf *cleats* commander-in-chief. Trump also forgot to take off his hat as he entered the building, and only remembered to remove it as he stepped into the spotlights.

It was indeed a sight. Trump obviously had not showered after finishing a round of golf. His hair, normally structured quite elaborately, instead stuck to his skull – hat head accentuated with some type of petroleum product. Platt pretended not to notice.

Platt had never really been political in his ministry, and he offered Trump a prayer that could hardly be described as pro-Trump. With one hand he raised his Bible, the other he placed lightly on Trump's back and asked God to offer wisdom for our leaders, and then included a bit that seemed almost subversive. As Trump kept his head bowed, Platt said: "Fools despise wisdom and instruction. Please, oh God, give him wisdom."

If Trump took offense at the possible slight, it was his turn to pretend not to notice. Platt finished, Trump thanked him, and then quickly left, without saying a word publicly, and within minutes was back in the motorcade, heading toward the White House. The whole thing lasted sixteen minutes, from the time Trump stepped out of the black Chevy Suburban, to the moment the cars and vans were rolling eastward toward the Potomac.

Was there much grief over what happened? Indeed there was.

And it was directed against … *David Platt*, by much of the evangelical Christian community, for his decision afterward to explain and sort of apologize for allowing Trump to come there in the first place. Platt's church is in northern Virginia, which even in 2016 was heavily anti-Trump, and which by 2019 was rabidly so. Even though the church is affiliated with the Southern Baptist Convention, Platt's congregation and Platt himself have little in common with the big, politically conservative mega-churches so popular in the South. Platt realized the offense many in his flock had taken, and wanted to make amends.

"My aim was in no way to endorse the president, his policies, or his party, but to obey God's command to pray for our president and other leaders," Platt wrote in an open letter posted on the church website. "I know that some within our church, for a variety of valid reasons, are hurt that I made this decision."

That not-quite-an-apology quickly made him the latest target of vitriol for the MAGA-hat brigade. And that group, of course, included actual, prominent leaders from the evangelical Christian community.

Jerry Falwell Jr., who endorsed Trump in early 2016 and who had attended the fall debates to explain to reporters just how much Christians loved him, had just fourteen words of advice for Platt, which he shared on Twitter: "Sorry to be crude but pastors like @plattdavid need to grow a pair. Just saying."

And what of Trump's attire in the house of the Lord? Not a peep. At least not from self-described evangelicals.

On its face, the incongruity is beyond absurd. While it is true that in the recent history of the White House, there has not been a more irreligious, amoral president than Donald J. Trump, his open flouting of the most basic standards of decorum was nevertheless mystifying. Trump, after all, wears a suit and tie to just about every public event he attends. That is his "brand," built over the years to give the impression that he was a brilliant and hard-working businessman, notwithstanding his actual business record, which was in reality quite dismal. Even in his time as president, Trump is almost always in the suit and tie uniform – at least partly to camouflage his expanding girth.

So why on earth would he show up in public looking like an uncouth slob – the sort of look that he openly derided when he saw it in staff like Stephen Bannon? The answer to that riddle lay in a decree by the son of the leading light of modern evangelical Christianity.

~ ~ ~

A year and three months prior to sweaty hat-head day at McLean Bible Church, the United States Air Force 89th Air Wing moved heaven and earth for Donald Trump.

An equinoctial gale was forecast to envelope the Washington, D.C., metro area with 50 knot winds, effectively grounding air travel. But the president was insistent. He had to get to Charlotte, North Carolina, no matter the cost. And so, the night before the wind came up, the 89th – the keepers of Air Force One, among other civilian transports – had their pilots take the big plane, the modified Boeing 747, from Joint Base Andrews in suburban Maryland, where it lives, and fly it 35 miles to Dulles International Airport in Virginia. Why Dulles? Because the capital city's much-scorned hub is the only one reasonably close to the White House with a runway that is both aligned in a northwest-southeast direction and also long enough to allow a fully loaded 747 to take off and land. That runway orientation permitted the jumbo jet to take off directly into the howling northwesterly, whereas the north-south runway at Andrews would have forced the plane to face a dangerous crosswind at takeoff and, even worse, in an emergency landing, had one been needed.

It was, nevertheless, quite the adventure getting up and above the layer of broken clouds, the heavy transport seeming to fall straight down at moments whenever the headwind would drop for an instant. After the bumpy climb out – according to the galley crew, the bumpiest they could recall – all was eventually fine.

But why would *this* president make a trip in these conditions? After all, his visit to a historic ceremony at Aisne-Marne Cemetery in France, near the site of the World War I Battle of Belleau Wood, where some 1,800 American soldiers had died, was canceled because it was raining. He avoided visiting a combat zone for nearly two full years after taking office because he feared for his personal safety. What was so important in North Carolina that he would accept this level of discomfort?

His connection to the voting bloc that put him in office, is all.

Billy Graham had died, and the funeral was to be that day in Charlotte. This was a big, big deal in the world of evangelical Christianity, particularly within the cultural right wing that has been the mainstay of Republican politicians for decades and whose support literally had lifted Trump to a position where the Russians and James Comey's letters were able to deliver him the victory. Trump was told that it would be noticed if he did not attend. And so it was that the big VC-25, as the Air Force designates the heavily modified jetliner, was pre-positioned in Dulles – at a cost to taxpayers of more than $100,000.

~ ~ ~

A year later, it was not Billy Graham who put a disheveled, unwashed and inappropriately shod president in a place of worship, but his son.

Billy Graham had famously tried to walk a bipartisan line, at least claiming to be supportive of every president and interested more in his spiritual well-being than his political one. Franklin Graham has not really bothered with that. After Trump had released the list of names from which he promised to choose a Supreme Court justice, Graham, like pretty much every white evangelical pastor, was fully on board.

That enthusiasm remained at a full boil two years into Trump's term, notwithstanding all the various and sundry unkind, uncharitable, un-*Christian* acts the president had managed to perpetrate, just in that short time. So it was on that Sunday, May 26, 2019, Franklin Graham declared in a video released on his Twitter feed: "I don't believe any president in the history of this nation has been attacked more than Donald Trump."

This included, presumably, Abraham Lincoln, who had been shot in the head for freeing the slaves and holding the nation together.

In any event, Billy Graham's son was declaring the following Sunday, June 2, "Pray for President Trump Day." He said 250 other pastors were joining him in asking every Christian in America to set aside a little time to pray for Trump one week hence.

The announcement generated some head-scratching outside of the right-wing Christian community, some rolling of eyes and shaking of heads among conservative Christians who broke from their brethren over Trump, but was more or less ignored by the public at large.

It was not ignored, though, by the intended prayee, who on the eve of Pray for Donald Trump Day responded to Graham on Twitter: "We will all stick together and WIN! Thank you Franklin."

Perhaps he believed that "re-tweet" of Graham's prayer call was sufficient, particularly with that promise of perpetual winning added in. Or perhaps what he posted online at 7:23 p.m. Saturday was completely forgotten by the following morning. Because at 8:58 a.m., his motorcade rolled off the South Lawn driveway to start the 26-mile trek to Trump's golf course along the Potomac River in northern Virginia.

At some point over the next few hours, though, someone realized that it was Pray for Donald Trump Day and Donald Trump was, instead, shooting eighteen holes, as is his wont on a Sunday morning.

It was only then that his team started working the phones. Fixing this was not as easy it might sound. Trump had an event scheduled for early that evening at Ford's Theater a few blocks from the White House, and then needed to get out to Andrews to fly to London. This did not leave much of a window. Most church services are Sunday mornings, not Sunday early afternoon. Even more problematic: Most churches were not participating in Pray for Donald Trump Day, which was confined to white evangelical denominations. The church closest to the White House, St. John's Episcopal, would not be taking part in Graham's hero worship. Nor would most Catholic churches and mainline protestant churches.

In the end, the call to McLean Bible Church was more about geography as anything else. Start at Trump National Golf Course in Sterling and plot a course to the White House and the route takes you directly past 8925 Leesburg Pike, the church's Tyson's Corner address.

The last-minute arrangements meant that Trump had no suit to change into. Or even a pair of normal shoes. And so, he went inside and onto the stage looking like he'd just walked off the 18th green. Which was, in fact, pretty much how it had happened.

His physical appearance – the clothes, the hair but particularly the golf cleats – was roundly criticized in the coming day or two. Except, of course, from one quarter: Evangelical Christians, who apparently saw nothing even in the least bit wrong.

"This is the sad thing. It won't matter," Kendal Unruh, a Colorado Christian school teacher and former Republican activist who led the unsuccessful effort at the 2016 convention to dump Trump as the nominee, told me at the time. "It doesn't matter how much he mocks our faith."

~ ~ ~

In a brief video touting a new book in 2018, Franklin Graham had a theory about how Donald Trump ended up in the White House. It didn't have anything to do with stolen emails or Vladimir Putin or even the political skills of Hillary Clinton. Rather, it was the doing of the Supreme Being.

126

"I think somehow God put him in this position," Graham said, explaining how Trump was such a poor politician, saying all the wrong things and angering so many people, that it *must* have been divine intervention for him to win. Then he added: "We need to get behind him and support him."

This was an idea that had already taken root among evangelicals, and Graham saying it no doubt added more legitimacy. In an interview with Christian Broadcasting in 2019, then-press secretary Sarah Huckabee Sanders repeated Graham's analysis. "I think God calls all of us to fill different roles at different times," she said from her office in the West Wing. "And I think that He wanted Donald Trump to become president."

The *Trump presidency as the Lord's handiwork* hypothesis, of course, raises a number of theological questions, the most obvious being: what exactly was He doing back in November of 2008, when Barack Obama was elected? Notwithstanding the logical cul-de-sac, though, is a more fundamental question: Of all the GOP candidates running in 2016, could not the God of evangelical Christianity find even one who was a more worthy vessel than the one He settled for?

For that has been the most striking paradox of the Trump era, this willingness of supposedly devout Christians to throw their enthusiastic support to a man like Donald J. Trump. His entire life has been a showcase of possibly the most un-Christian behaviors imaginable. A bullying aspect toward pretty much every other human in his orbit. A willingness to cheat business partners, contractors, suppliers at every turn. A thorough lack of charity. And a personal life that included carrying on with a porn star while his third wife was home nursing his fifth child. All of this was public and easily known to anyone paying even the slightest amount of attention. A less principled, more transactional human probably could not be engineered in a lab. And yet, there he was – beloved by evangelical Christians far and wide.

There were many a justification of this by evangelical leaders and their apologists in conservative media. They said ordinary Christians didn't really approve of his behavior, but were willing to hold their noses and accept it for the greater good. If he followed through on his promise to appoint conservative judges and thereby tilt the judiciary in a "pro-life" direction for decades to come, then it would have been worth it. Trump was like some of the leaders chosen by the God of the Old Testament, they explained. Like King Cyrus, whom God favored even though he was not really a good person, so as to accomplish His desired result.

This certainly sounds plausible. There sure were a fair number of Republicans making that exact argument about why, when it came down to Trump and Hillary Clinton, they wound up choosing Trump, because at least with him there was the chance of getting regulatory rollbacks, tax cuts and conservative judges, whereas none of those would be possible in a Hillary Clinton administration.

The problem was that even a cursory look at that thesis never really held up. Polling showed that halfway into his presidency, pretty much every single demographic group in the country disapproved of Trump. Blacks, Latinos, Asian-Americans, Catholics, Jews, college-educated white people. There was just the one notable exception: white evangelical Christians.

They not only approved of him, they approved of him by double-digit margins. Even after all the information that came out during the Mueller investigation, after all the news of the porn star hush money, the Muslim ban, the caging of children at the border, the separation of children from their parents, they still sided with Trump. Dig a little deeper, though, and it became clear that the support was not despite his actions, it was because of them.

None of these things, after all, had hurt people like *them*. White. Christian. Disproportionately rural. And hurting the "others" – non-white; in some cases non-Christian, but in other cases the wrong *kind* of Christian – was in fact a desirable goal, if it meant making the country more like it was in the golden era, way back in the late 1950s, before things started falling apart.

How did this world view square with the teachings of the Gospels? Love thy neighbor. Do unto others. That sort of thing?

It didn't, of course, which led to all sorts of analyses finding that evangelical Christians had lost their way in the age of Trump, had somehow been conned by this ultimate conman into forsaking their values in return for short-term political gains.

The explanations behind this were that Christians had finally gotten fed up with being treated with disrespect by the "elites" and had turned to Trump in desperation and, really, who could blame them, with the pervasive culture of "political correctness" that elevated every minority group and religion above Christianity and made it so you couldn't even say Merry Christmas any more without getting dirty looks and ....

At least, these were the explanations offered up on Fox News and Breitbart and AM talk radio and the other satellite campuses of the right-wing noise machine. They were the proofs in the thesis that Christians were really the victims here, and that Donald Trump was their understandable tool for striking back.

Not-terribly-distant history, though, offers a much simpler explanation.

~ ~ ~

In the shorthand of modern politics, evangelical Christianity is all about abortion. When *Roe v Wade* was decided in 1973 and abortion became legal just about everywhere, it served as the crystalizing moment for Christians who had lacked a unifying theme. In the coming years, they flocked to the Republican Party through Ronald Reagan, made themselves the litmus test of conservatism and, through groups like Focus on the Family and the Moral Majority, became the party's central and controlling voting bloc.

Simple, logical … and wrong.

As it happens, by the time abortion opponents recruited politically active Christians to their cause, "conservative" Christians were already mobilized, particularly in the South.

Their issue, though, was far less palatable than opposing abortion, which all but the most strident abortion-rights activists can agree is a morally understandable position.

Rather, the unifying cause for these Christians was the "right" to keep their children separate from Black children in the schools. This had become an issue following the *Brown v Board of Education* Supreme Court case in 1954, as the federal government, first under Eisenhower, then Kennedy, Johnson and even Nixon, had steadily increased pressure on public schools to end segregated classrooms.

While there were white parents who didn't want their children attending schools with Black children all over the country – recall the loud protests in Boston – the sentiment was especially strong in the South. There, groups openly organized to fight desegregation. The White Citizens Councils, for example. Parents who could afford to do so moved their children into private, Christian schools that would not accept Black kids. Far more astonishing, even parents who could *not* afford private school tuitions, or lived in places where there weren't any close by, pulled their children from public schools and invented their own private academies for them. Sometimes they took turns teaching. Sometimes they hired someone. Often that someone had absolutely no business in front of a classroom. It didn't matter. A lousy education for their own offspring taught by incompetent teachers was better than having them around Black people, even very small Black people.

What these parents then started demanding was state support for their new schools – in essence a way to reinstate publicly financed, segregated schools. In 1976, the IRS rescinded the tax exempt status of whites-only Bob Jones University in South Carolina, which enraged segregationists to the point of galvanizing them into action.

And it was on this issue that evangelical Christian political activism in the South was based, not abortion. That only came later. In fact, according to Dartmouth historian Randall Balmer, Republican operatives worked hard to persuade them that they were better off making their public focus an opposition to abortion, on which they could make a moral argument, rather than a return to segregated schools, on which they could not. To a large measure, the segregationists heeded that advice. Jerry Falwell became a national figure with his Moral Majority in the late 1970s and 80s. But before that, he ran one of those all-white "segregation academies," Liberty Christian Academy. In 1980, when Ronald Reagan spoke to 10,000 evangelicals in Dallas, he did not mention abortion even once (Reagan had actually signed into law the most liberal abortion rules in the country as California governor in 1967). But he did attack Jimmy Carter's IRS for going after "independent schools."

Given this history, of course, it all makes perfect sense why "the evangelicals," as Donald Trump calls them, would go for someone like Donald Trump, who has never evinced the slightest bit of interest in spiritual matters. In a candidates' forum in Iowa in 2015, he was lobbed softballs like: When are times you've asked for God's forgiveness? Trump responded that he's never needed to do that.

For genuinely religious Christians, this is apostasy. A foundational doctrine in modern Christianity is that all humans are sinners, even the best among us, and that we all need to ask God's forgiveness. Trump was mocked for not knowing that the New Testament book 2 Corinthians is known as "Second Corinthians," not "Two Corinthians." But Trump's admission that he is so prideful as to believe he does not need God's grace should have been the deal-killer for wear-it-on-their-sleeves Christians. Again, imagine Barack Obama saying that he never needed forgiveness. What might the reaction have been?

But for Trump, it was barely even a blip. Trump won a substantial share of self-described evangelical Christians in Iowa, even though he finished second. He won South Carolina easily, where they make up an even larger share of the Republican primary electorate, and then he rolled to enormous victories in the South on Super Tuesday, where Texas Senator Ted Cruz had assumed he would score decisive wins on his way to the nomination.

The Cruz camp seemed truly dumbfounded by this when it happened. Even years later, they pointed to polling showing that the more truly religious a person was, the less likely they were to support Trump.

Perhaps, but polling also showed that two years into his presidency, white evangelical Christians were the one and only slice of America that continued to approve of Trump – a full 69 percent, according to a March 2019 Pew survey. It was the underlying driver for every other demographic group in which he appeared to have a slightly positive or not-so-terribly-negative approval rating. White men, for example, appeared to still support Trump. But once you removed white men who described themselves as evangelical Christians, that number fell into negative territory. Same with white women. Or "working class" whites, those without a college degree. In each case, pull out that set who are evangelical Christians, and Trump's approval numbers plummet in that category.

The irony could not be richer. Those Americans holding themselves out to be more moral than everybody else constituted the only group in America who continued to support *the* most amoral man, if not the most actively immoral, to occupy the Oval Office in modern times.

Once it's understood that evangelical Christians are in fact the demographic group most gung-ho about building a wall along the southern border, the most supportive of breaking up migrant families as a deterrent to border crossings, the most eager about rounding up "illegal" immigrants and deporting them, then everything else fits into place. There is no longer a paradox to explain. No convoluted parables from the Old Testament are necessary to understand any of this. They like him for who he is, and he understands that and works to give them the "Make America White Again" policies that they desire.

~ ~ ~

Understanding the true motivations behind most self-described white evangelicals quickly illuminates other mysteries, as well.

The guns thing, for example. Jesus didn't really mention much about weaponry in the Sermon on the Mount, nor really anywhere in the Gospels. Yet it is at the top of the list of things that so many evangelicals rattle off about why they vote Republican: The Second Amendment and how liberals want to grab their guns.

For all the claims the National Rifle Association has made about its broad base of support, how it included people of all ethnic and economic backgrounds, all over the country, there has been for decades a great deal of overlap between its membership and the universe of white evangelicals. Beneath the layers of "I like sport shooting" and "hunting is a generations-old tradition" and "need to keep my family safe," there is a foundation of fear. There is truly a belief that the government will someday be in the firm control of *The Others*, and the only hope people like them have of maintaining their way of life is to remain heavily armed and constantly vigilant. When candidate Barack Obama talked about people clinging to their guns and their Bibles, this is what he meant.

For years, the NRA was able to exploit this fear to build itself a financial empire that only began to collapse, as fate would have it, when it started becoming enmeshed in the third piece of the evangelical Christian trinity, Russia.

~ ~ ~

It was one of Donald Trump's favorite complaints, whenever details from the Mueller investigation or one of the many congressional probes looking into his campaign broke into the news: "Russia, Russia, Russia!"

So it was trebly ironic when, in the end, the NRA's apparent demise as a political powerhouse during the Trump years also had its roots in Moscow. Bizarre though it may seem, the group that for decades had claimed to be the embodiment of America had, instead, over the last several years been in a deep courtship with Vladimir Putin's allies.

In 2015, a Russian gun group brought to Moscow top NRA leadership, where they were wined and dined, introduced to top government officials, including Foreign Minister Sergei Lavrov, and taken on a tour of a gun manufacturer. Granted, some of those who went had their own financial interests in mind – NRA vice president Pete Brownell was looking to expand the market for selling gun accessories that his family business produced, for example. Nevertheless, the breaking of bread with a regime led by a former KGB operative happily bringing back a dictatorship to his people would seem on its face at odds with the notion of preserving freedom – that thing the NRA supposedly had been doing for us Americans all that time.

Of course, those words "seem" and "supposedly" are doing a whole lot of work in that sentence. When the organization's mission is instead viewed as, in roughly equal parts, advancing the interests of firearm manufacturers by keeping elected officials in line while simultaneously maintaining a customer base fearful of losing its status in a changing America – well, then an alliance with Putin's Russia makes perfect sense.

Indeed, the more-than-a-little creepy level of admiration for Putin from white evangelical Christians and the NRA in recent years suddenly appears totally logical when you look at the country Putin is ruling. An almost exclusively white, "Christian" nation under a ruthless authoritarian who has systematically suppressed religious and sexual minorities. What Putin has in Russia is what a great number of Christian conservatives would like to see in this country – notwithstanding the rather obvious fact that Putin's behavior over the years is hardly that of somebody living by the lessons of the Gospels.

Of course, it's hard to argue that white evangelicals who are driven by fear and hatred of ethnic minorities and who proudly stand behind a man who has cheated thousands of contractors and suppliers, lies about nearly everything and whose personal corruption is the hallmark of his administration are themselves living by the lessons of Matthew, Mark, Luke, and John either.

What would Jesus do? Here is what he certainly would *not* do: support the likes of Donald J. Trump.

~ ~ ~

The Russian dictator has quite naturally reciprocated the show of love by the NRA by infiltrating it and working to use it for his own purposes.

As part of special counsel Robert Mueller's investigation, Russian-born Maria Butina was indicted and ultimately pleaded guilty to conspiring to act as an illegal foreign agent. Her "handler" appears to have been a Putin ally and banker named Aleksandr Torshin. Amazingly – or, actually, not so amazingly, when you get down to it – she even showed up at a Trump campaign event in Las Vegas and managed to ask him what he would do about ending sanctions against Russia.

True, increased public anger over mass shootings and the creation of groups like Michael Bloomberg's Everytown for Gun Safety to organize anti-gun Americans into an effective voting bloc had already started chipping at the NRA's dominance. But it was the gun group's dalliance with Putin's Russia that exacerbated financial problems created by lawsuits and the profligate lifestyle spending of its own leaders. Federal investigators were quite interested in how much of that $30 million the NRA spent to get Trump elected might have started out as rubles.

By mid-2019, the NRA was mired in internal battles over fraud accusations, a threat to its profitable gun-owners' insurance line and multiple investigations by federal and state authorities that, in the summer of 2020, even led to a lawsuit by the New York State attorney general to dissolve it entirely. The once-flush gun rights group's finances were such that it even had to stop providing free coffee to its employees at its Fairfax, Virginia, headquarters.

~ ~ ~

The demise of the NRA. The naked hypocrisy of white evangelicals. The open celebration by white nationalists.

Perhaps the one useful feature of the Trump presidency will be the clarity it has brought regarding that element of the voting base. When literal neo-Nazis marched in Charlottesville, chanting anti-Semitic and racist slogans and the president of the United States defended them and "Christian" conservatives stood with him and them, it was an illuminating moment.

Some academics and many progressives have long argued that the loudest faction of white evangelical Christianity in this country has for years been more about racial and ethnic animus than it has been about advancing the teachings of Jesus of Nazareth, which is literally what "evangelical Christianity" means. This comes into stark relief when contrasted to the adherents of other religions, even other strains of Christianity, who deeply disapprove of the president. Donald Trump has done pretty much the exact opposite of Jesus' teachings, behaving like a selfish, dishonest jerk his entire life, in ways so numerous that they have filled both biographies and courthouse dockets through the years. It turns out that for nearly 70 percent of white evangelicals, this was a feature, not a bug.

Again, the open admiration of Putin's Russia is instructive. Has Putin created a society that Christianity can be proud of? Does locking up critics, even having them murdered, jibe with *do unto others*? How about invading and annexing other countries? And what of the NRA's supposed ideals? Do they seriously believe that an aspiring dictator wants a heavily armed citizenry?

To the contrary, Putin has demonstrated exactly zero interest in living and leading according to the New Testament, notwithstanding the crucifix he wears around his neck, and has about the same level of commitment to Russians' "rights" of any kind, including the right to stockpile guns.

The admiration was, obviously, unidirectional. Putin had clear goals for himself and for Russia that installing Trump into the White House has helped him advance. Weakening NATO, increasing Russian hegemony over its former republics, hanging onto stolen territory, straining trade partnerships among Western allies – all of these things either help Putin's ambitions directly, or do so by degrading his adversaries.

And in each and every one of them, Putin was able to count on Donald Trump to do his bidding. Whether Trump was a willing participant or simply a dupe is an open question and yet, for all practical purposes, of little consequence. Whether Trump agreed to explicit requests made at their one-on-one meetings – Helsinki comes to mind; Trump confiscated the American interpreter's notes – or whether Putin has been able to manipulate him into carrying out his orders is not known. It could well be that he has promised the American president some future benefit. That long-sought Trump Tower in Moscow, say. It could well be that Putin has some leverage over him that allows him to coerce such behavior. It is possible, maybe even likely, that the American public will never know those answers. What matters is that, with or without leverage, Trump's actions – those that he took on his own; not those that Congress forced him to take, such as sanctions – invariably aligned with Putin's interests.

Disparaging the European Union, encouraging Brexit, unilaterally pulling American troops from Syria and, in late spring 2020, even announcing a drawdown of troops stationed in Germany all inured to the benefit of Putin's Russia. It is possible that Trump did not understand that. There are a great number of things Trump does not understand. But Putin sure does.

~ ~ ~

Way back in the summer of 2015, when much of America saw Donald Trump's presidential candidacy as an absurdist joke, I went to Atlanta to where Red State was holding their annual convention.

It happened to coincide with the first Republican presidential debate, which was the main reason I wanted to be there. Red State was oriented heavily toward religious conservatives, the evangelical Christians who have disproportionate pull in the Republican primaries. I was interested in how they would respond to Jeb Bush and Marco Rubio, the perceived moderates of the bunch, compared to Ted Cruz, who was already making it clear that he intended to be the most Christian candidate and win Iowa, South Carolina and then the southern states on Super Tuesday.

So it was stunning, then, that as the debate got rolling, the most raucous, most sustained whooping and cheering in the ballroom where the debate played on giant screens was for Donald Trump and his constant insults and attacks against the real Republicans on the stage. Even as the audience of Republican National Committee members and their friends booed Trump in Cleveland, actual Christian conservatives, the base of the party, who had gathered in Atlanta, applauded wildly.

They gave the rationales I would hear so, so many more times in the coming months. He tells it like it is. He's willing to fight *The Left*. He's not going to lay there and take it.

They knew about the multiple affairs and divorces, all the lawsuits, the lack of charity, the belittling demeanor – all of the un-Christian boorishness from this supposed billionaire. They didn't care.

Four years later, with hundreds of similar and even worse examples, they still don't. The rest of America may wind up turning on Trump this November, but he will, again, win evangelical Christians in a landslide.

8. Lemons to Lemonade

If Donald Trump was shocked the morning after the election to find himself headed to the White House, he had plenty of company in his own party, particularly those on Capitol Hill.

Republicans had controlled the House since the 2010 midterm elections, and took the Senate four years later. After two terms of a Democratic president and with a strong Republican field of candidates early in the 2016 cycle, congressional leaders were hopeful that a President Jeb Bush or Rick Perry or Scott Walker would finally be there to sign those bills the GOP had been itching to pass for years. All that had seemed to fly out the window as their top-tier candidates fell, one after the other, to the reality TV game show host's juggernaut through the Republican primaries. Hill leadership resigned itself to playing defense for another four or eight years under a second Clinton White House, only this time with an even more focused Clinton behind the big desk.

The big worry was that the Senate, too, would flip back to Democratic control, given how terrible a candidate Trump had proven himself to be. If that happened, the pressure on House Republicans would be enormous to work with Clinton and Chuck Schumer in the Senate, particularly if her victory margin were sizeable.

So when the results rolled in from the upper Midwest that election night, it was as if Christmas had come seven weeks early. Their dream of controlling both chambers of Congress and the White House had somehow, impossibly, come true anyway, despite Trump and his antics.

And then, not terribly long after the election, there came a Robert Redford-in-*The Candidate*-moment. Okay. Now what?

~ ~ ~

Had Walker or Chris Christie or Marco Rubio won, there would have been an agenda that any of their White Houses would have pushed hard in the first couple of months, while the election victory was still fresh and a mandate could still be claimed. That "honeymoon" period is critical for getting top election promises enacted while approval ratings are still in the post-inaugural surge. Ronald Reagan and George W. Bush were both able to pass big tax cut packages within a few months of taking office. On the other hand, Barack Obama, because of the Great Recession, had to delay his own campaign priorities and instead work to pass a stimulus bill to get money flowing again.

His major promise, a health care bill, had to wait, which, as it turned out, brought a host of negative consequences that might have been avoided if he'd had the luxury of pushing it through immediately – not the least of which might have been holding onto the House in 2010.

With Trump, Republican lawmakers faced a different problem: Their erstwhile leader *had* no agenda. At least one that made any sense or, at any rate, had much to do with Congress. "Make America Great Again" is not exactly a blueprint for legislation. Some of the things he did promise – making Mexico pay for a border wall; or pulling out of the Paris climate accord and the Trans-Pacific Partnership trade deal – he could do on his own, meaning Republican leaders in the House and Senate could pretty much ignore them.

As a matter of fact, as they realized pretty quickly, not only could they ignore a lot of what was coming from Trump's White House, but to have any chance of maintaining their sanity and compiling a legislative record to run on, they would pretty much *have* to ignore much of what was coming out of the White House.

Further, lacking any coherent direction from the western end of Pennsylvania Avenue, they went ahead with the generic Republican agenda that they had pursued for years, and did so with a vengeance. Which is to say: that pseudo-populist, anti-plutocrat, "drain-the-swamp" stuff Trump had been saying on the campaign trail to pick up Bernie Sanders voters? It all went right out the window.

A new surtax on the nation's wealthiest? Well, no, that was not going to happen on Paul Ryan and Mitch McConnell's watch. Trump may have talked about rebuilding the nation's highways and airports with a big "infrastructure" plan, but that wasn't part of the Republican agenda, either. Leaving Medicaid and Medicare untouched, as Trump had promised? As a matter of fact, cutting back on those entitlements had long been a Republican priority.

But in the days and weeks that followed, Republican leaders of Congress quickly learned what Vladimir Putin, white nationalists and the Christian Right already knew: Trump's lack of knowledge and inability to focus made him an easy mark for manipulation. Having won the White House with at best lukewarm enthusiasm from the Republican "establishment," Trump overnight became their useful idiot, too.

~ ~ ~

Capitol Hill Republicans got to work, in fact, even as Trump was flailing around his transition. Their first order of business: Undo whatever they could of the Obama administration's regulatory scheme.

Most Americans when they think about what the federal government does automatically think about laws. Laws that increase taxes or cut them. Laws restricting access to abortion or making it more available. Laws increasing or decreasing the speed limit.

In reality, laws, particularly major, far-reaching laws, are difficult to pass through Congress, which is why any presidency's biggest impact on the country is not through legislation, but through rules implemented by the executive branch agencies. These can be done in a matter of months, sometimes, and can have consequences on people's lives every bit as dramatic as new laws (indeed, most laws require that the affected agencies pass rules to implement them).

As it happens, Congress has the ability to nullify rules promulgated by an executive agency, provided that it pass legislation doing so within the first 60 work days of a new congressional session for rules that took effect in the final months of the previous session. Of course, a president has the ability to veto that legislation, so unless a rule is so overwhelmingly disliked by Congress that it can muster a two-thirds vote in each chamber for an override, there is little point in revoking a rule a sitting president has just implemented.

It is at the change of administrations, if both chambers happen to be of the same party as the new president and of the opposite party of the previous president, that there is a brief witching hour, during which the new regime can try to undo rules that had been implemented at the very end of the last one, if they hurry.

~ ~ ~

And hurry House Speaker Paul Ryan and Senate Majority Leader Mitch McConnell did, making it job one to reverse as many of Obama's regulations as they could. They began with the start of the new Congress, in the first week of January, with the House lining up bill after bill, dozens of them, to rescind rules protecting the environment, public health, consumers and labor.

It is important to keep in mind the underlying reason for this. Republicans as a party in recent years have consistently favored their business community donors over the public in the area of government regulations. This was not always the case. Richard Nixon, after all, championed the Environmental Protection Agency in 1970. Nixon also signed into law the Clean Water Act of 1972, just weeks before his landslide re-election and in the same year he approved creation of the Consumer Product Safety Commission. George H.W. Bush signed into law the Clean Air Act of 1990 that helped reduce acid rain by regulating smokestack emissions.

But especially after the Obama years, two straight terms of relatively aggressive rule making, the business community was screaming for a rollback of regulations, and every Republican candidate running for president had promised to comply.

In other words, the Great War on Obama's Job Killing Regulations would have been waged with energy and enthusiasm to beat the statutory deadline regardless of which particular Republican had won that year. Trump, naturally, took all the credit for those bills undoing the Obama administration's work, as if he had thought of the idea himself.

He loves the imagery of signing things – bills, proclamations, executive orders; it doesn't really matter. He scrawls out his name in magic marker in his peculiar, up-and-down penmanship, then holds it up for the cameras to admire. All this legislation rescinding Obama regulations, a total of 16 bills, to be exact, gave him that many more opportunities to show off his signature on an official presidential document.

Those rescinded rules ranged from making it harder for mentally ill people to buy guns to preventing internet companies from selling data about their customers to forcing industries to keep better track of worker injuries to preventing the killing of bear cubs in their dens in federal wildlife reserves.

Trump signed every one that got to his desk, and was proud to do it.

"We've eliminated more regulations in our first year than any administration has ever eliminated," Trump bragged at a Republican congressional retreat the following February.

~ ~ ~

On the opposite side of the Capitol, meanwhile, Senate Majority Leader Mitch McConnell was taking the lead on the single greatest windfall that Trump's unlikely win had generated for Republicans: the ability to load up the federal judiciary to the gills with ultra-conservative judges.

Regardless of what happens with Trump's re-election bid, this one element will clearly be the longest lasting achievement of his administration. Federal judges, even at the trial court level, are appointed for life, and the ones Trump was appointing were selected in large measure for their youth. Men and women – mainly men – in their forties, with some even in their thirties. These people could, in theory, still be issuing rulings and writing appellate level opinions four decades from now, the equivalent of five two-term presidencies.

Democrats could win control of both chambers of Congress and the White House in, say, 2040, and pass all manner of legislation regarding corporate governance or emergency fossil fuel regulations – and watch it get overturned by judges approved under the term of a failed businessman and former television game show host more than 20 years earlier.

Progressives who never understood the big deal conservatives made about federal judges before the 2016 election probably understand it better now.

This play for control of the judiciary is, as we've already seen, the final arrow in the quiver of religious conservatives and their secular, white nationalist allies who long for the "Father Knows Best" America of the 1950s. A voting populace so fickle that it would elect Barack Obama – twice! – could not be counted on to turn back the tide. Only unelected judges, therefore, could be relied upon to see this sacred mission through.

There are obvious plot holes in this story line, of course. People's views change as they get older, so a judge in his early forties might well be a very different person in his late fifties. More important, the judiciary has at times slowed societal change in America, but it has not reversed it. Slavery wound up going away, *Dred Scott v Sandford* notwithstanding.

Indeed, to focus on the social changes the Republican voting base wants to reverse is to miss the key point on this issue.

What's happening here has far less to do with *Roe v Wade* than it does with *Chevron v Natural Resources Defense Council.*

~ ~ ~

That 1984 Supreme Court ruling gave executive agencies broad power to make rules, provided they did not go against express mandates from Congress. Even though the particular rule in Chevron was written by the Reagan administration and opposed by environmentalists – it relaxed pollution standards – conservatives have been trying to limit its scope ever since, worried about the power it gave liberal presidents to impose mandates on industry that could not be stopped in court.

The implications of this case for big businesses whose executives and major shareholders have a disproportionate influence on federal elections are obvious. There is a reason senators grilling judicial nominees, especially appellate court nominees, spend so much time asking about "Chevron deference." It is the same reason a group of conservative, pro-business lawyers created the Federalist Society nearly four decades ago: to recruit and screen potential judicial nominees so as to have a list ready to go for whenever a Republican president is in place to fill vacancies. True, many of the group's members also happen to oppose abortion, but the driving force is the business community, not pro-lifers.

An even bigger misreading of the judges issue than its underlying motivation, though, is to ascribe any measure of the plan's success to Trump, however often he claims it and his apologists insist he deserves it. Had he failed to deliver on that pre-election quid-pro-quo, Republicans would have impeached him in a heartbeat.

Trump's involvement in the appointments themselves has been minimal, at best. Yes, it is technically his signature on the document that sends a nomination to the Senate. But apart from that, he knows almost nothing about them.

This was, recall, by design, and a feature that was critical to him getting elected. Had he not agreed to this arrangement – in which he promised to literally rubber stamp whatever names the Federalist Society would give to him – he would never have been in a position where Russia and James Comey's letters could have put him over the top.

On May 18, 2016, his campaign published a list of names that he promised to choose from to fill the Supreme Court vacancy that McConnell had refused to let Obama fill. All had been pre-approved by the Federalist Society. It was the most openly, brazenly transactional piece of politics on something that had once been thought of as a high, almost sacred honor. Trump could not have cared less about that. He was told that this is what the Christian base wanted in return for their support, and he said no problem.

The Federalist Society, of course, has been the unofficial screening committee for Republican judicial appointments for decades. And pretty much any of the other Republican candidates running in 2016 would have been fine with that same list of names, and would have done it without the explicit quid-pro-quo arrangement that conservatives demanded of Trump. In any case, once a nomination was in McConnell's hands, Trump's part in the process was finished.

McConnell had already, single-handedly, re-written the rules on how the Senate confirmed federal judges. Using the excuse that Democrats had slow-walked George W. Bush's judicial appointments during the second half of his second term, McConnell began slowing Obama's appointments in the second half of his first term, after Democrats lost their supermajority in that chamber in the 2010 midterms (they had technically lost it in the special election to fill the seat left by the death of Massachusetts Senator Ted Kennedy, when Republican Scott Brown unexpectedly won).

When Obama, to Republicans' shock, won a second term, McConnell made it his mission to grind the process as close to a halt as he could manage to keep to a minimum the number of judges Obama would be able to appoint during those second four years. This infuriated Democratic Majority Leader Harry Reid to the point where in November 2013 he pushed his caucus to change the rules – invoking the so-called "nuclear option" to end the filibuster for appointments to the trial and appellate levels of the federal judiciary. Meaning that instead of needing 60 votes to confirm a judge, Reid and his Democrats would only need 51. The 60-vote threshold was retained for Supreme Court justices. More on that later.

For the remainder of 2013 and all of 2014, Reid made it *his* life's mission to ram through as many Obama judicial appointments as he could. The Senate still retained its ordinary cumbersome rules, notwithstanding the end to the judicial filibuster, so McConnell could force each judicial confirmation to burn a number of Senate work days going through all the necessary steps when unanimous consent to shorten the process does not exist. Despite this, Obama was still able to get a fair number of judges on the bench – 305 by the end of 2014.

That was when Obama's second midterms delivered to Republicans a majority in the Senate, giving McConnell control of that chamber, and setting the stage for the GOP judge machine that came to be in Trump's first years.

~ ~ ~

McConnell and the new Republican president were different in just about every way, except for one: A complete lack of shame.

In Trump, that trait reveals itself in greed, vulgarity and hypocrisy in just about every area, from his interpersonal relationships to a complete amorality when it comes to his word. In McConnell, it manifests as a laser focus on whatever particular goal is at hand, and a willingness to do whatever it takes to achieve it.

Upon Trump's ascension to the Oval Office, everything was in place to remake the federal bench according to McConnell's vision, and the valves were turned to open the pipeline, pretty much starting right off with the biggest one, a justice to replace Antonin Scalia on the Supreme Court. The Federalist Society, working through longtime Republican lawyer Don McGahn now ensconced in the West Wing as Trump's White House counsel, settled on a name to push to Trump: Neil Gorsuch, a judge on the 10th Circuit Court of Appeals, which covers four western states.

McConnell wasted little time with any pretense. Harry Reid, his Democratic predecessor, had left in place the filibuster for Supreme Court appointments, on the rationale that a position on the highest court deserved to have nominees that could win a supermajority of the Senate. McConnell eliminated it within three months of Trump taking office to pave the way for Gorsuch's Supreme Court nomination to win approval with just Republicans.

That precaution made the second of Trump's Supreme Court nominations, that of Brett Kavanaugh, even remotely possible, as he wound up having trouble getting 51 votes, let alone 60. Despite damaging testimony against him from high-school classmate Christine Blasey Ford and some unanswered questions about his personal finances, McConnell muscled him onto the bench. Because that is what McConnell does.

Did the process of loading up the courts with hard-right conservatives, including some who were given a rare "not qualified" rating by the American Bar Association, diminish the federal judiciary? Probably. Did the Kavanaugh confirmation taint the Supreme Court with the odor of partisanship? Almost certainly. Did McConnell care? Almost certainly not.

~ ~ ~

Undoing as many Obama regulations as possible and remaking the federal courts for a generation made up two of the three great accomplishments Republicans boast about under Trump. The third – and last – was tax cuts.

"Last" because it represents the only significant piece of legislation Republicans managed to pass in their two years of complete control of Congress before losing the House in the 2018 midterms. Indeed, that it *was* the only significant piece of legislation to have passed played a role in losing the House in the first place.

Republicans, of course, did not believe that would be the case. Many continue to argue that had they failed to pass it, their drubbing that November might have been even worse.

No matter. Suffice to point out that the rush to pass the tax cuts package in the final months of 2017 was, more than anything else, driven by the complete disaster that became of Republicans' attempt to repeal the Affordable Care Act in the first half of 2017. The details of that adventure will be examined in the next chapter.

But the key take-away from that episode necessary to understand tax cuts is the one that congressional Republicans learned from it, to wit: They needed to minimize, to the greatest extent possible, Donald J. Trump's involvement in their legislation. Yes, he technically was president of the United States and his signature was necessary for something to become law. But he knew nothing about policy and wasn't interested in learning anything, yet generally held strong views anyway so that his involvement was likely to muck things up and they were much better off just passing what they wanted and hoping for the best.

And that is precisely what they did with their remaining top priority, tax "reform," as they preferred to call it. In fairness, a large number of Democrats, Barack Obama included, agreed that corporate tax rates in the United States should be reduced to bring the code more in line with other industrialized countries. But most of those Democrats, Barack Obama included, believed that tax rate reductions should be balanced with the elimination of some deductions and credits for businesses so as not to reduce the amount of money coming into the Treasury. In fact, Obama had proposed exactly that in his second term.

That Republicans were not in the slightest bit interested in such legislation was revealing. Yes, they wanted to reduce corporate tax rates, but even more important, they wanted that to generate a windfall for those corporations – which are, coincidentally enough, disproportionately owned by the rich people who fund their campaigns.

This was something pretty much all Republicans could support, even those who did not want to mess around with Obamacare or Medicaid or any other social welfare program, and GOP congressional leaders set about making it happen. They understood that the calendar was not their friend. They needed to pass something before December 2017 slipped into January 2018 or risk having nothing at all to show for their first year of all-Republican control heading into the congressional midterms. The key was leaving Donald Trump out of the picture, knowing that he would make wild, uninformed public statements about anything he was involved in.

And, so, leave him out of the picture they did. By working with White House economic adviser Gary Cohn, a former Goldman Sachs investment banker, and Treasury Secretary Steven Mnuchin, a former hedge fund manager and film producer, they had partners who were both knowledgeable about the policy and in agreement about the ultimate goals. Trump's only real involvement appears to have been to make sure that limited liability companies such as his – that simply "pass through" income to their owners – would also benefit from the business tax cut.

McConnell and Ryan relatively quickly pulled together a bill cutting the top corporate tax rates nearly in half. Sure, there were a number of Republican lawmakers from swing states who needed to be assuaged with cuts that also helped middle-class and poor people, so some of their demands were thrown in, as well – the doubling of the child tax credit, for example, from $1,000 to $2,000, which was the only element in the plan that provided any meaningful benefit for most taxpayers. (Unsurprisingly, all of the provisions that help non-rich people expire after 10 years, while the corporate rate cuts are forever.)

McConnell and Ryan had all along intended to use a procedural shortcut to let them pass their tax cuts with just 51 yes votes in the Senate – ordinarily, 60 are needed – thereby eliminating the need to win over even a single Democrat. And so it was that, despite predictions that the legislation was too complicated and too unwieldy to move in such a short time frame, they did what it took to pass it.

As it turned out, casting a vote to cut taxes is never really all that difficult in Congress, particularly when your party has claimed – falsely and against all evidence going back five decades – that they will pay for themselves in higher economic growth. (That thesis, by the way, was disproven yet again, as annual deficits jumped to $1 trillion by 2019, thanks to revenue forgone by the tax cuts – even before Trump's mishandling of the coronavirus tanked the economy.) It also turned out that as long as Trump's business entities were able to share in the spoils, Trump personally did not seem to care that the package bore little resemblance to what he had promised as he ran for the presidency.

Back in October, 2016, Trump released his "contract" with voters that outlined his various promises. In the area of tax cuts, Trump pledged that his plan would give middle-class Americans a 35-percent reduction in their taxes. At other times, he had even spoken of a tax *hike* on rich people such as himself.

Yet when the "Tax Cut and Jobs Act" reached his desk, it had been designed to give rich people such as himself the lion's share of the benefit – some 23 percent of the total tax savings would be going to the top 1 percent, according to an analysis by the Joint Committee on Taxation. (Had it not been for the insistence of increasing the child tax credit by Florida Senator Marco Rubio and others, the plan actually would have resulted in higher taxes for lower-income workers with large families.) Trump ignored all that, and instead leapt right in to tout the legislation as pretty much the best thing the country had ever seen. He even began claiming – falsely, naturally – that it was the biggest tax cut ever. "Just as I promised the American people from this podium 11 months ago, we enacted the biggest tax cuts and reform in American history," he said in his 2018 State of the Union speech.

Republicans had gotten exactly what they wanted: A package of tax cuts that helped corporations and their wealthiest donors while providing little or nothing for the bulk of Trump's working-class voting base. And Trump had done not a thing to stop them.

~ ~ ~

As it happened, the Tax Cuts and Jobs Act (Trump frequently told his audiences that he had wanted to call it the "Cut, Cut, Cut Act" – and apparently believed this was a brilliant idea.) was the one and only consequential piece of legislation to pass in the two years of all-GOP control.

In fairness, an election year is always a more difficult time to pass significant bills than non-election years, but the lack of even an attempt to pass important legislation was both amazing and yet, upon further reflection, not terribly surprising. After all, with a president exhibiting a toddler-level attention span, there was never real leadership for anything.

On "infrastructure," for example, Trump could have put Democrats in a tough spot by offering a roads, bridges and airports package that would have helped people in both liberal and conservative areas. But with his fleeting interest in the topic, "infrastructure week" instead became just a recurring inside-the-Beltway joke to lampoon the self-inflicted disaster *de jour* in the Trump White House.

Helping the hundreds of thousands of undocumented immigrants who were brought into the country as children obtain legal status could have been another easy bipartisan legislative win for Trump. It would have fulfilled a campaign promise, it would have been the right thing to do, and, early on, he could have readily traded it for billions in funding for his beloved wall along the Mexican border. Even that never came close to reality. Trump simply did not care enough to make it happen, and so his top immigration aide, notorious anti-immigrant Stephen Miller, was able to strangle the "Dreamers" bill in the crib.

True enough, the ramming through of judges by McConnell's Republican Senate continued apace heading into

152

Trump's re-election, as did the dismantling of environmental, labor and consumer regulations by Trump's executive agencies. It's important to remember, however, that neither of those operations had a thing to do with Trump personally, apart from the occasional piece of paper that was put before him to sign. More to the point, neither did they have anything to do with the so called "Trump agenda."

~ ~ ~

Which gets to the major irony of the Trump years, the one that confounded Democrats and liberals who could not understand why congressional Republicans would not break with a president who was quite plainly deranged. Some of them, sometimes even a decent proportion of them, expressed their unhappiness with Trump's frequent and unhinged outbursts in interviews, public remarks and, most often, on Twitter. Despite this, when it came time to vote, they almost always toed the party line. Democrats were beside themselves: *They criticize him but they never vote against his agenda!*

What these critics misunderstood completely was the nature of those votes. For all intents and purposes, there *was* no Donald Trump agenda. True, there was an occasional vote for a particular thing that Trump really wanted. His allies in the House in the first two years, for instance, tried to put funding for the border wall that Trump had promised into various spending bills, but could not get much support from leadership, let alone from enough Democrats in the Senate, to make that happen.

But the tax cut bill that Republicans all supported? That was something they had been pushing for years. A tax "reform" package resembling the one that passed in late 2017 under President Trump would have passed under a President Jeb Bush or a President Rick Perry or a President John Kasich. Cutting taxes is modern Republican orthodoxy. The only thing amazing about the one that passed was that they were able to get it into law despite all of Trump's various and sundry nonsense.

Similarly with the Federalist Society judges and the regulatory rollbacks. To consider votes for them as votes "for" Trump fundamentally misreads how things worked. Yes, Trump frequently took credit for all the judges he had appointed. (On numerous occasions, Trump would recount to his audiences how Obama had failed to appreciate the importance of the federal judiciary and had foolishly left a huge number of vacancies for Trump to fill. Yes, he is that delusional.) That doesn't mean he had either interest or much knowledge in how or why that was happening.

As for an actual Trump agenda, as in the things he ran on that made him distinct from the other Republicans running?

Well, Trump promised to renegotiate trade agreements to make them favorable to the United States. That has not happened, because Trump did not as a candidate and does not now as president understand how international trade works. He has instead started trade disputes with China, Canada, Mexico, Germany, India, France, the entire European Union, and so on, with no good result. He promised to give parents all over the country vouchers that they could use at private schools. That didn't happen, either, perhaps because of a failure to understand that almost all school funding comes from local and state taxes, and the federal government has virtually no role in the matter. And his biggest, most often repeated promise? That was to build a massive, 30-foot concrete wall along the Mexican border, and to make Mexico pay for it. That also did not happen. Trump never even dared to broach the topic with Mexican leaders. By his third year in office, he was instead raiding the military budget – paid for with American tax dollars, not Mexican pesos, to get at least some miles built in time for his re-election.

Indeed, in his three and a half years in office, there was probably just a single real vote on even one piece of Trump's "agenda" in the Senate – a more meaningful test than in the House of Representatives, where votes on bills that are not destined to go anywhere are typically decided on purely partisan lines. In the early spring of 2018, Trump – which is to say, Stephen Miller – was insisting that lawmakers pass his immigration package – which is to say, Stephen Miller's immigration package – that would have appropriated $25 billion for a border wall, set strict limits on legal immigration, ended the visa lottery program that ensures people from poorer countries have the opportunity to emigrate here and also created a path to citizenship for the illegal immigrants who had been brought into this country as children. Mitch McConnell's Senate had been looking at several proposals, including a bipartisan plan sponsored by eight Republicans and seven Democrats. McConnell decided to allow votes on four of them. The bipartisan compromise proposal, which provided the wall money but over ten years, created the citizenship pathway for the "DACA" undocumented immigrants, but did not restrict the existing immigration programs, received 54 votes – just six shy of the 60 needed to move forward. The Trump-Miller plan? It got a total of 39 votes. The fewest of any of them.

In other words, the progressives complaining about Republicans who agreed that Trump's character was deficient but who nevertheless voted eighty or ninety or ninety-nine percent of the time for Trump's "agenda" had it backwards. They were voting for their *own* agenda all those times. And, yes, they were genuinely upset about Trump's latest temper tantrum or bout of racism or Putin-philia. Because with each of those, he made it ever more likely that he would make their party lose control first of Congress and then the White House.

And so the Republican establishment came to appreciate what the Christian Right and white nationalists had already learned. Yes, Trump would be their useful idiot, too, but only for as long as they could keep the scam going.

Which, as it turned out, wasn't all that long. And, with any bargain with the devil, there comes a time to pay up.

9. Live by the Idiot, Die by the Idiot

In the summer of 2019, there came to be public perhaps the most useful documents for describing the Trump presidency. Confidential memos written by Britain's ambassador to the United States were leaked as part of Brexit-related, internecine backstabbing in London to a pro-Brexit, pro-Trump tabloid.

Why this happened, and why that particular messenger was chosen to carry it out, is not really of interest outside the United Kingdom. What is important is that the author of these notes – some to then-Prime Minister Theresa May, some to Foreign Office colleagues – had absolutely zero interest in personally attacking Donald Trump. He wasn't a Democrat hoping to damage the president politically. He wasn't a Republican hoping somehow to replace him. He wasn't part of a "special interest group" or even a journalist trying to score some attention.

Rather, it was a 40-year career diplomat doing his job: writing accurate, unvarnished assessments of the national leader at his assigned posting, with the belief that they would be read only by those few people with whom he was sharing them, for their use in shaping their own nation's foreign policy.

And what Sir Kim Darroch wrote was devastating: That the president of the United States was an inept and insecure buffoon running – if that was the right word for it – a dysfunctional White House and administration. That his presidency could very easily end in "disgrace. That he would, if he were to win a second term, further damage military alliances and trade relationships. That if the United Kingdom was counting on a major trade agreement with the United States post-Brexit, that would be a serious miscalculation.

Trump, to no one's surprise, immediately lashed out at Darroch with his typical insults. He proclaimed that "we" wouldn't be dealing with him anymore, and again repeated his criticism of Darroch's boss, Theresa May, for failing to listen to Trump's advice on how to negotiate a good Brexit deal. May's government put out statements criticizing the leaks but insisting – correctly – that the job of its diplomats was to provide honest appraisals for their colleagues. But when her likely successor, Boris Johnson, refused to support Darroch in a televised debate that weekend, Darroch tendered his resignation.

The ignominy of such a public downfall notwithstanding, Darroch could at least enjoy the happy result that he no longer had to be afflicted by Donald Trump's exhausting chaos as part of his daily life ever again. Which was a fate that the Republican Party that had nominated him for the presidency three years earlier could only dream about.

It is certainly true that Republicans had their way with a significant piece of the regulatory framework – ramming through industry-friendly appointees to enable the gutting of safety and environmental regulations. They absolutely got the massive cohort of young, doctrinaire conservatives who would be the pro-business, anti-labor, anti-voting rights judges they had dreamed about for decades. They even got the giant tax cut bill slashing the rates on corporations nearly in half and then, kind of for fun, cutting personal rates on individuals, as well – even though the net effect was to make trillion dollar budget deficits the new normal, even before Trump's inept response to the coronavirus sank the economy.

For these long-sought goals, though, there was a price, and it was a steep one: Having to defend the unhinged guy at the other end of Pennsylvania Avenue. The guy who also happened to be the leader of their party.

~ ~ ~

Let's agree, right up front, that describing Trump with words like "unhinged" turns off a lot of Republicans and, frankly, a great number of people generally who don't pay much attention to politics. It seems insulting, childish, disrespectful toward the office of the president of the United States, and so on. And in the case of every other president in modern times, such criticism would be warranted.

However – in the case of Donald J. Trump, of Queens, New York, the 45th president of the United States, that criticism is just plain uninformed. "Unhinged" is actually being kind. Reckless, narcissistic, endlessly mendacious, breathtakingly ignorant, foundationally immoral – all are more precise, but each somehow incomplete. His is a damaged psyche, through and through, as cynical a human being as might be imagined, who truly seems to believe that everyone else is as dishonest and corrupt as he is, and who lives by the maxim: Do unto others before they can do unto you.

So, yes, most people feel a reflexive need to defend someone who is being unfairly picked on. The instinct behind that is good and decent. But rest assured, Donald Trump is not that someone. And the damage he has inflicted upon his country and his party is deep and quite likely lasting.

This was clear even before the first week of January, 2020, when Trump ignored ample warnings that a deadly disease was rampaging through a major Chinese city and could easily make its way to the United States.

Paying attention to this sort of thing is the singular job of a president. The occupant of the Oval Office has access to the world's most extensive intelligence gathering network, updated constantly. So what did Trump do with it?

Literally, nothing. He played golf. He staged rallies for himself. For the first five days of January, he had no intelligence briefing scheduled at all, and only had nine scheduled the entire month.

Mitch McConnell and his Senate Republicans, ironically, had the perfect opportunity to rid themselves and the country of this menace a few weeks later, thanks to Trump's attempts to coerce Ukraine into investigating the Democrat he most feared in 2020. His extortion scheme, which used $391 million in military aid as leverage, had gotten him impeached by the House, and if 20 Republicans in McConnell's Senate had gone along with the 47 Democrats, Trump would have been finished.

Yet, save for Mitt Romney, they did not. Trump's attempt to cheat his way to re-election put Richard Nixon's efforts to shame, but McConnell and his Republicans did not care. Mind, their agenda of slashing regulations and loading the courts with right-wing judges would have continued uninterrupted under President Mike Pence. In effect, Trump's abuse of power and resulting impeachment had given McConnell the serendipitous opportunity to rid his party and his country of him, once and for all.

But McConnell and his crew chose to live with their useful idiot. And in the following months, upwards of a hundred and fifty thousand of their fellow Americans have died because of that idiot as a direct result.

~ ~ ~

There are Republicans who no doubt truly believe that slashing taxes without slashing spending, letting businesses do what they will with as little government interference as possible, installing a judiciary intent on restoring the social order of the 1950s, and dismissing climate change as a problem for another day is – somehow – in the best interest of the country. It's possible to question their judgement on these issues without having to question their integrity.

What's harder to explain away is their willingness to place the nation in the hands of someone as profoundly ignorant, fundamentally dishonest and, at his core, as truly mean-spirited as Donald Trump. The majority of them understood his attributes full well by the time he had hijacked their party.

Indeed, after wishfully thinking he would disappear on his own through the summer and autumn of 2015, both the presidential candidates who had already dropped out as well as those still in the race were loudly articulating his many flaws by the final months of that year. The Republican Party at that moment was still their party, not that of the boorish game show host who had crashed it. It did not require clairvoyance or any special analytical skills to correctly predict what a Trump presidency would be like.

Jeb Bush called Trump a "chaos candidate" and warned that, should he win, Trump would be a "chaos president." Marco Rubio called him a conman, and said that if he hadn't been born rich, he would have been on the streets of New York, trying to con tourists into buying counterfeit Rolexes. But the single most impressive takedown of Trump was offered up by none other than Ted Cruz on the day Trump essentially clinched the GOP nomination by winning the Indiana primary.

"I'm going to tell you what I really think of Donald Trump," Cruz began in what wound up an extended, minutes-long rant. "This man is a pathological liar. He doesn't know the difference between truth and lies. He lies practically every word that comes out of his mouth. And in a pattern that I think is straight out of a psychology textbook, his response is to accuse everybody else of lying.

"He accuses everybody on that debate stage of lying. And it's simply a mindless yell. Whatever he does, he accuses everyone else of doing. The man cannot tell the truth, but he combines it with being a narcissist. A narcissist at a level I don't think this country has ever seen.

"Donald Trump is such a narcissist that Barack Obama looks at him and goes, 'Dude, what's your problem?' Everything in Donald's world is about Donald. And he combines being a pathological liar – and I say pathological because I actually think Donald, if you hooked him up to a lie detector test, he could say one thing in the morning, one thing at noon and one thing in the evening, all contradictory and he'll pass the lie detector test each time. Whatever lie he's telling, at that minute he believes it."

Was Cruz upset that day that Trump had beaten him? Absolutely. Did that make what he said any less true? Absolutely not. Indeed, Cruz was not revealing any secrets that afternoon that the leaders of his party did not already know. The fact of it was, the actual Republican candidates and the Republican party leadership could have, had they put their minds to it, saved the country from Donald Trump. They chose not to.

Instead, they chose to believe the nonsense they were privately selling to donors and reporters: that Trump, in the off-chance that he should win, was manageable. That his staff would be old Republican hands who would moderate his nuttier impulses and that Congress would provide an effective check. And that, besides, he was a successful businessman, so he couldn't be a complete idiot, right?

The answer to that question seems plain as day now, given the literal carnage Trump's failures with the pandemic have wrought.

In truth, though, it was pretty apparent just three months after Trump had stood on the Capitol steps and taken the oath of office that Republicans had inflicted a true menace on the country and the world. The triggering event during that spring of 2017?

Like so much about today's Republican Party and its new leader, it had to do with the previous occupant of the White House, and the party voting base's unrelenting antipathy toward him.

~ ~ ~

By the time he left office, Barack Obama was still Black. Just as Black as the day he announced his candidacy, just as Black as the day he made history when he won the presidency, and the day four years later when he won it a second time.

And after his departure, this Blackness continued to present a big problem for Republicans.

Because for the previous seven years, they had promised their voters that they would make repealing the Black guy's signature legislative achievement their top priority when they back took control of the White House. Now, unexpectedly, they had it – but their guy sitting at the big desk had absolutely no plan on how to deliver on that promise. Unlike the serious candidates who had put out plans that at least made a show of replacing "Obamacare" with something that wouldn't strip health care coverage from tens of millions of people, Trump had nothing. In his speeches and interviews, he had promised – absurdly – that he would give everyone who wanted it far better coverage at a much cheaper price.

Not surprisingly, he made it clear in early meetings with Republican congressional leadership that he expected *them* to figure it out. After all, they had been running on repealing the law for a lot longer than he had. In fairness to Trump, that was, in fact, true. It's also true that Republican lawmakers had laid little or no groundwork to replace it when that opportunity arose.

That also should not have come as a surprise. The political genius of the Affordable Care Act was that it was based on a model drawn up at the ultra-conservative Heritage Foundation and then implemented in the state of Massachusetts – by a Republican governor. On a policy level, it inflicted on its recipients some of the worst aspects of the workplace-centered, insurance-based model, but that was the tradeoff. It effectively put Republicans who insisted on a "free-market" approach to health care for people who couldn't afford it into a box. If they pushed ahead to repeal the ACA, they would have to admit that a market-based approach was not the best way to go, even as they actively took health insurance away from people who only recently had, for the first time, gained access to it.

Truth be told, while there were some Republican lawmakers who as a matter of principle opposed the idea of government helping poor people get health care coverage, far more of them

162

wished the whole thing could just go away. With Obama no longer in office, and with more Americans learning, for example, that the law prohibited insurance companies from refusing coverage because of pre-existing conditions, the ACA was getting more and more popular as time passed. Actually repealing it would bring serious downside risks that had not been present when the Republican House could pass repeal bill after repeal bill knowing full well that Obama would never sign any of them into law.

Republican leadership, though, felt hemmed in by their perennial promise to *lift the yoke of Obamacare off the American public* to follow through and deliver, and so they did. House Speaker Paul Ryan, in fact, decided it should be the first major piece of legislation, before even the tax cuts, because of some convoluted logic having to do with how the ACA repeal would save money that could then be applied to reduce the tax cut bill's cost.

It was an enormous miscalculation – but one that, ironically, wound up sparing the country the horrors of other, yet-to-be-imagined Trump-backed legislation by helping Democrats win back the House in the 2018 midterm elections.

~ ~ ~

Because as they finally started looking at the practicalities of "Repeal and Replace," it did not take long at all for Republicans to start running up against the same Rubik's Cube that had bedeviled Democrats eight years earlier when they were trying to pass the health-care bill in the first place. Eliminating the requirement that every American buy insurance meant either making coverage for poorer families unaffordable for them or exorbitantly expensive for the federal government. No amount of "eliminating the state lines" – as Trump had famously advocated in one GOP debate – was going to magically make it better.

Making things even harder was the so-called "Freedom Caucus" in the House, a group of some three dozen hardliners from safe Republican districts who had become famous for making former Speaker John Boehner's life miserable by opposing any type of compromise with Obama. This same pack now enjoyed direct access to Trump's White House. The repeal bill Ryan's team had come up with eliminated requirements that Americans buy insurance and that employers offer it, but did not get rid of the subsidies for poorer people. Freedom Caucus members called it "Obamacare Lite" and threatened to scuttle it by withholding their support. That in turn forced Ryan to call off a floor vote – one that Trump had demanded because he was getting impatient and wanted a "victory" to brag about in his first 100 days.

Indeed, that right there was Trump's primary role through the entire health-care process: An agitated spectator angry that things were taking so long. Trump at various times told Republicans he didn't want to pass anything that hurt the elderly or his supporters in states that he won – apparently not understanding that it was mathematically impossible to satisfy all his various requirements. In a February speech to the National Governors Association, Trump told his audience: "Now, I have to tell you, it's an unbelievably complex subject. Nobody knew that health care could be so complicated."

Nobody, that is, except anyone who had spent even five minutes studying the issue. His admitted ignorance notwithstanding, Trump continued riding herd to get his braggable victory, and ultimately pushed the House to approve a bill essentially gutting protections for people with pre-existing conditions and which the nonpartisan Congressional Budget Office estimated would take health-care coverage away from 24 million Americans. Sure, he had promised as late as January 14, exactly six days before his inauguration, that every American would be covered by his plan. Just over three months later, he evidently had forgotten that pledge, because he immediately demanded that House Republicans come over to the Rose Garden to celebrate this great victory.

Whether Trump understood that getting a bill through the House is literally less than half the battle is unclear, but he certainly came to appreciate it seven weeks later. McConnell had been no more successful in crafting legislation fulfilling the GOP promise of "better" health care for less money than the House had, and eventually scheduled a vote on a do-nothing placeholder bill designed merely to get the issue into a House-Senate conference committee. And that set the stage for Arizona Senator John McCain, diagnosed with terminal brain cancer, to return to the Senate floor to deliver a dramatic, wee hours of the morning thumbs-down – the deciding "no" vote killing McConnell's bill.

~ ~ ~

Trump, predictably, was incensed by McCain's decision. The naval aviator who had spent five and a half years in a Hanoi prison during a war Trump avoided thanks to fake "bone spurs" quickly became one of Trump's favorite villains in his tweets, in interviews, even in speeches, both campaign related and "official" White House remarks.

Republican leaders in the House and Senate, meanwhile, took away their own lesson from the debacle: They could not count on even halfway competent leadership from the White House. Whatever they truly wanted done, they would have to do themselves, and hope for minimal interference from Trump. The tax cut package that they rammed through in the remaining months of 2017 proved out this strategy.

It was, alas, their only significant legislative victory in their two years of total control of the legislative and executive branches. Far, far more of their collective time and energy was spent dealing with the sheer wall of nonsense rolling uphill from 1600 Pennsylvania Avenue each and every day.

At this point in the discussion, Trump's defenders typically point to the changes his election brought to the world of business regulation. And it is true that Trump's appointees to the various executive branch agencies (a good many of them from the political orbit of Vice President Mike Pence) were able to undo or weaken a great number of environmental, worker safety and consumer protection regulations. Trump frequently bragged, in fact, that his gutting of regulations was perhaps more profitable for businesses than his tax cuts had been.

Of course, regulations undone or weakened by one president can be reinstituted or strengthened by the next. Indeed, the aggressive nature of Trump's deregulation regime is almost certain to bring an even more far-reaching response from the next Democratic president.

Lasting change comes through bills that can get through the Senate, which by its rules requires a three-fifths supermajority. So here is the damning top-line: Republicans and Trump could not manage a single piece of significant legislation that reached that threshold in the two years they had full control of the process. Even their much-vaunted tax cut bill was done using a gimmick that allows passage of budget-related bills under "reconciliation" rules that only require a simple majority. That is the reason, in fact, that the tax cuts that benefit ordinary wage earners expire after ten years – because those budget rules require such a "sunset" if the bill will be generating a deficit in that tenth year. (Again, the tax cuts that benefit corporations and their owners, which is to say, "rich people," are permanent.)

So what, then, was the cost to Republicans for medium-term ownership of the federal judiciary, a temporary rollback of regulations, and a business tax cut bill?

Their ability to get anything else done. Their further loss of control of their party to a narcissist with the impulse control of a toddler. Their pummeling in the midterm elections in which they lost control of the House and, despite the most favorable map in decades, won a net gain of just two seats in the Senate.

Their future.

~ ~ ~

All of this was both foreseeable and, indeed, had been foreseen by a good number of people, including Republicans, prior to his election. Trump's behavior, which veered from merely ridiculous to downright depraved, had been on full display during his decades in New York City and then for a year and a half on the campaign trail. Despite this, more than a few made the argument that in the unlikely event he won, the gravity of the office would weigh on his shoulders and modify his behavior accordingly.

That this was complete and total wishcasting, not grounded in any knowledge of his personality whatsoever, became crystal clear barely 24 hours after taking the oath of office, when Trump went to CIA headquarters, stood in front of their sacrosanct memorial to fallen officers, and … began complaining about his media coverage and straight-up lying about the size of his inaugural crowd. A few hours later, he demanded that his press secretary, as his first official interaction with the media in his new job, repeat and embellish on this lie – thus poisoning his relationship with the White House press corps just hours into the administration.

The nonsense has never really let up. Trump claimed that his predecessor had wiretapped his office and residence at Trump Tower (more precisely, he accused Barack Obama of having ordered his people to "tapp" Trump's phones during "the very sacred election process," but, whatever). He insisted that millions of people had illegally voted in the 2016 election, all of them for Hillary Clinton, apparently, thereby robbing him of a popular vote victory. He proclaimed during a visit to a new, state-of-the-art aircraft carrier that the electromagnetic aircraft launch system was too complicated – you had to be "Albert Einstein" to understand it – and decreed that it and every other new carrier would be retrofitted with World War II-vintage steam catapults.

He claimed that the European Union was invented for the sole purpose of taking advantage of the United States, as were some actual European countries. He decided that Denmark should sell Greenland to the United States. Then, when the Danish prime minister predictably called the idea absurd, he called off, via snitty tweet, a state visit to Copenhagen that had been planned for months.

During National Security Council briefings on approaching hurricanes, he demanded to know why they could not destroy the storms in their infancy off the coast of Africa using nuclear weapons. He loudly and repeatedly bragged about his "Space Force," apparently not realizing that for decades the Air Force had already been running a Space Command – and apparently believing that his "new" creation would station actual armed astronauts in orbit.

Some of the worst insanity, predictably, took place overseas, during organized meetings with other world leaders. What began with incredulity that America could have elected someone this preposterous gave on to attempts to manage him with flattery to, by year three, barely concealed irritation.

The 2018 meeting of the G-7 in Biarritz was a perfect showcase. Having given up on persuading a man who during his campaign had called climate change a Chinese hoax, French president Emmanuel Macron didn't even bother trying to craft a joint communique on the issue, in hopes of avoiding another scene. Trump managed to wreck the meeting anyway, by arguing long and hard that the largest democratic economies in the world should re-admit Russia, even though Vladimir Putin had done nothing to end his occupation of Crimea, the reason they had booted him from the group in the first place.

Trump then took his advocacy for Putin public in a rambling news conference, where he claimed – falsely – that Russia had been kicked out because President Obama had gotten mad about being "outsmarted" by Putin. (This outsmarting was demonstrated, presumably, by sending tanks and troops into Ukraine.)

Trump also used the setting to push for hosting the 2020 G-7 at his struggling golf course in Doral, Florida. Asked about the propriety of directing the government to choose a venue that would enrich him personally, Trump claimed – falsely, but also laughably – that holding the event there wouldn't make him any money.

Just a couple of weeks later, of course, the G-7 mess was all but forgotten because Trump had generated a brand new mess that drew all the attention instead. As Hurricane Dorian grew to Category 5 strength and began edging across the Bahamas, Trump posted a statement on Twitter warning residents of Florida, Georgia, the Carolinas and, inexplicably, Alabama, which was not at all in the forecast path of the storm.

Why Trump decided to include Alabama in his warning is probably not worth trying to psychoanalyze. He does love drama, and has frequently expressed his fondness for Alabama because it voted for him, so it might have been as simple as wanting to write them into the episode. In any case, his tweet likely would have been quickly lost in a stream of similar meaningless nonsense had he simply let it go.

Of course, he could not, and argued for ten full days that Alabama *had* been in danger of getting hit by the storm at the time he sent his tweet, and then demanded that his White House and his entire administration join him in this Orwellian double-think exercise. The most bizarre turn was when he displayed at an Oval Office photo opportunity a Hurricane Center forecast map – on which an extra, and false, semi-circle had been embellished using a black Sharpie.

It cannot be overstated, just how reckless Trump's baseless decision to include Alabama in that tweet was. National Hurricane Center forecasters are scrupulously precise in their public advisories, and with good reason. Large-scale evacuations have both inherent risks and opportunity costs. You don't want to encourage people to leave an area unless they absolutely have to. At the same time, once you've determined a storm is likely to hit, you want them to heed that warning immediately and without reservation.

Hurricane Center meteorologists don't even like "windshield wipering" a long-range forecast track first in one direction and then back the other over a period of days because of the confusion that creates, and here the president is straight-up inventing a nonexistent threat?

Of all the absurd fabrications Trump had disseminated to that point, none had put lives at risk as immediately and as obviously as "Sharpie-gate." Meteorology and emergency management professionals saw this at once, and quickly raised a collective outrage.

But what did White House staff, political appointees at the National Oceanic and Atmospheric Administration and some Republican lawmakers do? Incredibly, they defended Trump, backing up the outlandish and false claim that forecasts had originally threatened Alabama.

It was breathtakingly shameful – and, unsurprisingly, passed largely with a shrug, and a oh, well, that's just Trump.

~ ~ ~

Halfway into his term, it got to where administration officials were basically advising federal agencies to ignore Trump and just do their jobs.

Such a thing sounds ridiculous, of course, because it is. And yet, in reality not only was it somewhat doable, but it actually was done on a fair number of instances and across the administration. Despite Trump's repeated statements about wanting steam catapults on the new aircraft carriers, for example, the Navy did absolutely nothing to act on his whim. Defense Department officials were similarly able to drag their feet for months after Trump announced on Twitter that he was banning transgendered people from the military. Border Patrol officers ignored Trump's request to ignore federal law and refuse to process asylum claims from migrants they had detained.

Sometimes, though, this ad-hoc continuity of government strategy was simply not practicable, as Trump by the nature of his office was central to the debate.

An example that crystalizes the problem came in the late summer of 2019, when Trump's trade war against all comers combined with the come down from the tax cuts' sugar high the previous year led to clear warning signs of an economic downturn, from two straight months of negative growth in manufacturing to rounds of layoffs to a big downward revision in the employment number.

It's unclear whether Trump the self-proclaimed genius businessman understood or appreciated the significance of any of these. Some of his economic and political advisers did, and started bringing him possible steps to avert a slowdown in his re-election year, including temporarily reducing the payroll tax.

Naturally, reporters got wind of this, leading to an absurd – but completely typical – 48 hours. On Monday, August 20, the *Washington Post* published a story about the payroll tax cut plan, leading to an immediate denial from the White House – only to have Trump personally and quite casually concede the following afternoon that, yeah, they were talking about cutting the payroll tax as a way to juice the economy. Only to have Trump personally but, this time, with a good deal of agitation, insist that no, they *weren't* discussing a payroll tax cut because, really, the economy was so strong that why would they need one?

And the day after that, reacting to a speech by the Federal Reserve chairman in which he explained why tinkering with interest rates could not fix the ongoing uncertainty in international trade, Trump had a complete meltdown on Twitter, wondering if Jerome Powell or China's Xi Jinping was the worse "enemy." The stock market reacted as expected. At day's end, after the Dow had fallen some 600 points, Trump tried to make a joke out of it, blaming it on market reaction to Massachusetts congressman Seth Moulton, who had dropped out of the Democratic presidential race earlier that day.

For all but that segment of his supporters who were going to back him no matter what for those various other reasons detailed previously, this was a stunning display of incompetence. *This* was the guy in charge of leading the country through the coming recession?

The remnants of the Republican Party that remained more loyal to that institution than to Trump personally, meanwhile, could only watch in dismay as Trump used similar management skills in politics.

As Tim Alberta reported in his book *American Carnage*, Trump was livid about Minnesota Republican congressman

Erik Paulsen's attempts to distance himself from Trump in hopes of retaining his suburban seat. One night – *after* his political affairs shop had refused to do so – Trump posted a tweet giving Paulsen a full-throated endorsement leading into the 2018 midterms. Paulsen was likely going to lose anyway, but Trump's backing was the last nail in the coffin.

Knowing when to stay out of races, knowing when one's involvement would do more harm than good, has been a fairly basic political skill for presidents going back decades. That Trump would rather have a Democrat in that seat than a Republican who refused to kiss his ring speaks volumes about his interest in the Republican Party and, more important, his capacity for rational, strategic thinking.

~ ~ ~

Finally, any explication of Trump's nonsense must touch on the endless, constant, exhausting stream of falsehoods coming out of the man's mouth. It is, easily, the defining feature of his presidency. Which really should not have been a surprise, because it was also the defining feature of his candidacy and, when you think about it, the defining feature of his adult life.

Indeed, Trump's endless lying was well known to anyone paying any attention, from the time he came down his escalator. Cruz's exit-from-the-race tirade, though, hit upon an important point. While many, maybe even most, politicians spin and obfuscate the facts and on occasion might even straight-up lie to achieve a particular objective, Donald Trump's dishonesty is on a whole different level. Falsehoods seem to roll off his tongue almost for the sheer fun of it.

Trump lies about everything, from the momentous to the trivial, and with wearying regularity. Trying to keep up with them all quickly became a tedious chore for journalists, a soul-crushing burden for Republicans who were invariably asked about them, and simply mind-numbing for average Americans.

Trump lied about the size of his inaugural crowd. He invented "millions" of illegal votes by illegal aliens that gave

172

Hillary Clinton her popular vote victory. He made up Japanese officials who supposedly told him that Democrats wanted the country to fail, just to make Trump look bad. He told the leader of Pakistan that the prime minister of India told Trump he wanted him to mediate an agreement on Kashmir – forcing the Indian government to put out, within minutes, a statement denying that Narendra Modi had said any such thing.

He has lied repeatedly about the status of the border wall that he promised Mexico would pay for. (He lied several times that Mexico *was* really paying for it, when, in fact, Mexico has not sent us a single peso.) He lied that China was paying the tariffs he had imposed on imported Chinese goods. He lied many, many, *many* times that he had successfully passed the VA "Choice" Act, when it was really Barack Obama who had done that.

He lied about steel plants opening up. He lied about auto plants opening up. He lied about how NATO works, and other member countries "ripping us off." He lied about the origins of the European Union. He lied about NAFTA as well as the revised version of it he rebranded USMCA, but which, in reality, is still basically NAFTA.

"He lies like he breathes," a former top White House aide once told me.

Were he not president of the United States, figuring out the *why* behind the incessant falsehoods might have been a fascinating but ultimately unimportant psychological case study. Unfortunately, he *is* the president of the United States, which means there have been and continue to be actual consequences for all his dishonesties.

Eventually, people get tired of getting lied to and just start out assuming that little or nothing you say is accurate. By the third year, a CNN poll showed that only 28 percent of Americans believed that information they were getting from the White House was all or mostly true. (How even 28 percent could believe that is probably worth its own book.) For foreign governments, the falsehoods combined with the general chaos of dealing with the White House meant normal relationships were nearly impossible, at least at the leadership level. Militaries, foreign services and intelligence agencies continued the basic information sharing and coordination lower down at the non-political staff levels. But, just like in America, by year three the efforts by the various prime ministers and presidents to flatter and cajole and barter had largely ended, and the focus had instead shifted to simply getting through one more year.

It's difficult to overstate how much damage all of this had on America's standing in the world and our relationship with traditional allies. Trump's penchant for ill-considered policies, exacerbated by his compulsion to lie about them, meant that the United States pulled out of a comprehensive trade agreement uniting the Pacific Rim nations of Asia and the Americas. Cozied up to the dictator of Russia while simultaneously disparaging NATO. Emboldened and made excuses for the ruthless ruling family of Saudi Arabia. Legitimized and encouraged the murderous dictator of North Korea. Pulled out of the first major international agreement on climate change. And abandoned a working nuclear agreement with Iran. Naturally, Trump all the while claimed to all who cared to listen that each of these actions represented major victories for the United States.

America will be suffering the effects from all of this for years or decades to come, nowhere more so than because of Trump's fervor to deny evidence of human-caused climate change. At the direction of Trump and his appointees, the United States government silenced the work of our own scientists laying out the dangers posed to the nation by spiking carbon dioxide levels in the atmosphere, all to please a stubborn ignoramus who during his campaign dismissed the problem as a "Chinese hoax."

Far too often, far too many Americans have been willing to give Trump a pass on the idea that *they all lie.* And, in fact, that's what Trump and those who want to emulate him want everyone to believe. That everything is corrupt. That everyone lies.

Well, they don't. In my three and a half decades in journalism, I have never encountered anyone who was as regularly and shamelessly dishonest as Donald J. Trump, and that includes my years covering serial killers in Daytona Beach and Florida legislators in Tallahassee.

The fact is, most politicians don't lie. They spin and play word games and obfuscate and change the subject – but they do their damnedest not to say anything that is provably untrue, because to lose their credibility is irrevocable and quite possibly a career ender. At least, that's how it used to be in pre-Trump times.

And that is where we need to return, once he is gone. Self-government cannot survive in a post-truth world. Maybe having elected someone like Donald Trump will be what it takes for people to realize that.

~ ~ ~

So often Republicans point to Trump's victory in a circular proof that assumes he must have had a brilliant, carefully thought-out strategy to win, otherwise he couldn't possibly have become president. They continued with that model in justifying his trade war or his alienating longtime allies. "The genius of Trump..." they would begin.

But three and a half years in, if one thing has become clear about him, it's this: There is no "genius" to Trump. What you see is all there is. And if it seems as if he's acting and talking and tweeting like an idiot, well, there is a reason for that. As one anonymous White House aide told the *New York Times*, no, he is not playing multi-dimensional chess. He is merely eating the pieces.

By the end of Trump's second year in office, more and more observers were openly discussing Trump's behaviors in ways that had only been whispered about earlier. He was more frequently repeating himself in his remarks, using the incorrect word for a similar-sounding one, forgetting names of people he was meeting with or had just recently been speaking with. In a

175

span of a few days in early 2019, Trump seemed unable to form the word "origin," and instead kept saying "oranges." He said that his father, rather than his grandfather, had been born in Germany. He called Apple CEO Tim Cook "Tim Apple," and then later tried to explain it away by claiming he was speaking quickly and using shorthand.

By 2020, Trump grew increasingly defensive about his physical and mental slips. During his infamous Tulsa rally in June, he spent long minutes rationalizing his difficulty walking down a ramp following the West Point graduation ceremony and his need for two hands to drink from a glass. Weeks later, he gave a bizarre interview boasting of his ability to say "person, woman, man, camera, TV" as proof of his mental acuity.

Given his age, and his father's history, early signs of Alzheimer's would not be surprising in the least – nor something to be ashamed of. In any presidency, it would raise difficult questions of competence and judgment, given the demands and responsibilities of the job.

In Trump, the questions were downright terrifying. Because Trump, even in his prime, exhibited none of the characteristics normal people would like to see in the commander of the world's most powerful armed forces. In his 40s, he would call journalists using an invented name to claim he was sleeping with supermodels. In his 50s, he got up on stage at a ribbon cutting for a nursery school for children with AIDS, taking credit for supporting it even though he had never donated a dime to the cause and had not even been invited to the event. And throughout his entire adult life, he routinely cheated his contractors, forcing them to sue to collect payments he had promised in writing.

Over-the-top dishonesty, shameless egotism, rampant narcissism, a complete absence of morals – this was behavior you might expect to see, and still be appalled by, in an immature 11-year-old boy. It is what happens when parenting has failed to instill the most basic of societal norms. Donald Trump at age

74 has the impulses of a toddler, the sense of fair play of a middle-school bully and the guile of a delinquent teenager.

It should have come as little surprise, then, how he reacted when a crisis struck that would have bedeviled the most competent of managers.

10. Donald Trump Meets the Coronavirus

The president of the United States suggested that people inject disinfectants into their lungs.

If there was a single moment that clarified everything about Donald Trump and his presidency, and the bargain Republicans made four years earlier when they put him in office and then again early in 2020 when, despite his impeachment, they kept him there, that was it. Thursday, April 23, 2020, at 6:14 p.m. in the evening.

No, it wasn't the worst thing that Donald Trump did during his pandemic response. It probably doesn't even make the top ten worst things. In truth, the self-evident stupidity in even suggesting such a thing objectively made it, ironically enough, probably one of the best things in his response, because it revealed ever so much about him and his entire administration, and all in just a few seconds.

Yes, he had said many, many, *many* idiotic things before, as documented ad nauseam previously, but never about something that was literally killing more than a thousand Americans a day. Suddenly in a span of 200 words over 66 seconds, the emperor's new clothes disappeared on live television.

No amount of spinning and explaining could undo what was now obvious: Clearly, Donald Trump had no business whatsoever to be in that job.

~ ~ ~

That April 23 press conference, of course, merely provided the quick and easy sound bite for television networks and, later, the attack ads.

Obviously, no rational human being was going to mainline Lysol on Donald Trump's say-so. (Just to protect themselves from legal liability from Trump supporters who never got the memo and continue to take him both seriously *and* literally, manufacturers of Lysol, Dettol and other cleansers quickly put out warnings to consumers that, no, under no circumstance should they inject, ingest or otherwise introduce these branded cleaning products into their bodies.)

The inane statement – made complete by the pained efforts of coronavirus coordinator Deborah Birx, a medical doctor, to maintain a neutral expression – was just the final breaking point. The true dereliction of duty on the pandemic had begun four months earlier. As Trump was facing impeachment in the House and then a removal trial in the Senate, what remained of his attention was focused on his trade agreement with China, which he saw as critical to his re-election.

Because while Trump had spoken frequently and with authority about the United States' trade relationship with the rest of the world for several decades, the fact remained that he had and continues to have a fundamental misunderstanding of the topic. In his mind, if Country X imports more from Country Y than it exports to Country Y, that is proof that Country X is "losing" that trade "battle," and that Country Y is "ripping off" Country X.

This is, of course, just plain silly. Just about every American has a negative balance of trade with the local supermarket. Does that mean that Wegmans and Publix and Albertsons are ripping us all off?

As in so many other areas, Trump sees the world around him as a zero-sum game. There is no such thing as a mutually beneficial partnership. There are only winners and losers. And in Trump's telling, China had been "ripping us off" for years, because of horrible presidents who had let it happen.

Trump's views on international trade back when he was a reality game show host or a New York City condo salesman really had no import, one way or the other. But as president, he decided he would get tough on China and imposed huge tariffs on Chinese imports, which had enormous repercussions both for American manufacturers suddenly facing higher costs for raw materials as well as for consumers buying everything from clothes to electronics. What Trump apparently had not counted on was the Chinese retaliating with tariffs of their own – targeted specifically at the people whose support Trump would need to win a second term: farmers in the Midwest.

China's import tax on American soybeans and pork, among a host of other products, was designed to hit Trump where it hurt, and hurt it did. Yes, he has bragged about how he used the billions of dollars "collected from China" – a lie; American tariffs are paid by Americans – to make the farmers whole with bailouts – another lie; the bailouts came nowhere close to making up for their lost earnings.

Generally speaking, farmers have tended to vote Republican, as most people in rural America have done in recent decades. But as the trade war dragged on from the summer of 2018 for a full year and into the autumn before Trump's re-election, farmers' support for Trump began to soften. Michigan and Pennsylvania, two of the three "Blue Wall" states that Trump had unexpectedly won by the narrowest of margins in 2016, were already looking like they would vote against Trump this time. And Wisconsin, the most rural of the three, was suffering from a wave of farm bankruptcies on top of a manufacturing slump, with exporters facing retaliatory tariffs, all thanks to Trump's trade war. What's more, Iowa, which he had easily won but whose big pork industry had been hammered by Chinese tariffs, was starting to look shaky, as were other agricultural states.

So as the end of 2019 neared, Trump's zeal to ink a "deal' with China and boost farm exports began rising exponentially, until it essentially became all-consuming. So all-consuming, in fact, that when China in the final stages of the negotiations insisted on a provision triggering a reopening of talks in the event of a natural disaster or other unforeseen event, Trump's team either didn't notice or didn't care.

~ ~ ~

Imagine if George W. Bush had downplayed not just one warning in one intelligence briefing about al Qaeda wanting to hit the United States, but more than a dozen of them. Now imagine that rather than downplaying the warnings in his intelligence briefings, he had simply refused to take the briefings in the first place.

Starting in mid-December, with that odd demand by China for *force majeure* language in a trade agreement, through alarms from Taiwanese authorities in late December about a mysterious outbreak of pneumonia-like cases on the mainland through explicit warnings from U.S. national security agencies starting in early January, Donald Trump ignored it all.

International trade agreements between major countries are not like business contracts between two companies. "Act of God" provisions are not generally included in them, because nations, particularly large ones like China, are big enough that a flood or a drought in one region is likely not going to affect the country's overall ability to import and export. The massive Trans-Pacific Partnership negotiated under Barack Obama did not have one, for example. Nor did the deal with South Korea updated under Trump.

The fact China was demanding one should have been a clue that something was up. And, of course, something *was* up. In late October or November, strange cases of a SARS-like respiratory illness were cropping up in Wuhan. Reports about it were circulating in the area by late November and more broadly by mid-December. One person close to the White House told me the United States had an extremely good idea what was happening and when, because one of our intelligence agencies had a source actually working in Wuhan's virology lab.

By the end of December, the new disease was out in the open, with Taiwanese health officials warning the world that China was experiencing a bad outbreak. Both the Centers for Disease Control and the Department of Health and Human Services were on high alert over the New Year's break. The *Washington Post* reported that the disease and its risk to America made its first appearance in Trump's "President's Daily Brief" in the first days of January.

It was followed by multiple additional warnings throughout that month in the package of intelligence reports of threats from around the world collated each morning specifically for the president's eyes, with the warnings getting more dire as the weeks progressed.

Of course, a "President's Daily Brief" is only useful if the president reads it.

~ ~ ~

During the first five days of January, Trump was wrapping up his two-week golf vacation at his Palm Beach resort, Mar-a-Lago. Not a single intelligence briefing was scheduled during that entire stretch. The first one on his schedule in 2020 was January 6. He took only nine that whole month, and that was three times as many as he received in February. Meaning that in the 60-day period that saw the explosion of the world's worst health crisis since 1918, Donald Trump took just 12 "daily" intelligence briefings.

To be clear, getting intelligence briefings and taking appropriate action based on them is not a minor, if-there's-time-for-it sort of thing for a president. It is literally his damned job.

Not for Donald Trump. He has loads of time for watching television, hours and hours of it, each morning, and then tweeting about what he has just seen. He has time to call his rich friends from New York, the members of his various golf clubs, to solicit their thoughts on everything from Kim Jong Un's intentions to the actions of the Federal Reserve, but he doesn't have time for the singular responsibility that a president, and no one else in the federal government, is entrusted with?

Every previous president going back to the start of the PDB has taken the role seriously. George W. Bush received his early each morning. Barack Obama preferred to have it loaded onto his iPad by 6 a.m. each day, and would have read it by the time of his in-person briefing later in the morning. Trump, on a good week, will receive two briefings, and even those, as the *New York Times* reported in an extraordinary warning to the public from the intelligence community, are contentious affairs with Trump frequently telling briefers that they are wrong and going off on random, time-wasting tangents.

And as January proceeded, Trump made it plain that he was not interested in hearing about a deadly viral outbreak in China, particularly since asking questions about it could jeopardize his all-important trade deal. And so it was that on January 13, 14 and 15, with top Chinese officials on White House grounds for the signing of his trade agreement, no one in the Trump administration pressed them for details about the worsening situation in Wuhan.

In fact, Trump's fixation with the agreement, which rolled back some tariffs in exchange for China agreeing to purchase large quantities of farm goods, continued even past the signing. When asked about the virus in the coming weeks, Trump continually praised China and its leader, Xi Jinping, personally.

On Jan. 22, the first day Trump spoke publicly about the coronavirus, he told Fox News there was nothing to worry about. "It's all taken care of. And China is working very hard on the problem. We spoke about it and China is working very hard on it."

"China has been working very hard to contain the Coronavirus," Trump wrote two days later in a Twitter post. "The United States greatly appreciates their efforts and transparency. It will all work out well. In particular, on behalf of the American People, I want to thank President Xi!"

Even two months later, Trump still had only kind words for China's dictator. "Look, I have a very good relationship with

President Xi and they went through a lot. You know some people say other things. They went through a lot. They lost thousands of people. They've been through hell," he told reporters on March 24.

And when he was not praising China, he was pretending that the virus wasn't a problem at all, or that it might have been a problem if he hadn't successfully stopped it from coming into the country with his China travel ban that he instituted despite opposition from other countries, the Democrats and even many in his own administration.

"We're doing an awfully good job, I think, with what we're doing," he said in late March.

Unsurprisingly, virtually all of his claims were false. By the time he finally imposed restrictions on people entering the United States who had been in China during the previous two weeks, nearly fifty other nations had by that point taken that action. U.S.-flagged airlines had already stopped flying from China on their own because of the outbreak. And his own experts were not only telling him to institute travel restrictions from China, but from Europe as well, where the disease was rapidly spreading by mid-January. Trump and some of his Cabinet members resisted the European restrictions because of the shock they would send through the markets.

Indeed, Trump's entire response from January 22, when he first mentioned the outbreak, right through March 16, when he finally appeared to take it seriously, seemed guided by just two motivations. The first was to avoid spooking the stock market, which Trump seemed convinced was going to bring him a second term with its historically high valuations. And the other was to avoid angering Xi Jinping, who could on a moment's notice renege on his promise to buy American farm products, which would threaten Trump's standing in several key states.

The heights of absurdity to which Trump took this became manifest in late February, when he lost his mind over comments by the CDCs' Nancy Messonnier on a conference call with reporters. She matter-of-factly stated that she had discussed the near-certain arrival of the disease in the United States with her children, and the changes it would require in all of their daily lives, and how she thought all Americans needed to similarly prepare.

Trump was on his way back from a visit to India when he heard of her statements and the stock market's resulting plummet, its second in as many days. He demanded that his top aides get out and retract her warning. Upon his return on February 26, still unhappy that his "all is well" message was not taking hold, he made his first very foray into the White House briefing room since taking office for an unplanned news conference, where among many other things, he offered this prognosis: "When you have 15 people, and the 15 within a couple of days is going to be down to close to zero, that's a pretty good job we've done."

Over the coming two weeks, Trump was in the briefing room on a near daily basis. He continued to claim that the virus was under control, that he had done a phenomenal job, and that all would soon be back to normal, with the soaring economy he had created with record-low unemployment and a record-high stock market, and that he would roll to an easy re-election. In this time, he continued his rallies – including one in South Carolina where he claimed that all the concern about the virus was another Democratic/news media "hoax" ginned up to hurt his re-election – and hosted gatherings of hundreds at Mar-a-Lago. (One of those wound up an impromptu coronavirus party, with a number of people in the entourage of visiting Brazilian president Jair Bolsonaro testing positive in the coming days.)

It was only on March 16 that his attitude seemed to change, after both an in-person plea from Fox News' Tucker Carlson to take the pandemic seriously followed a week later by estimates from his top health officials showing that, in the absence of any preventative measures, as many as 2.2 million Americans would die. So it was on that Monday that a noticeably sober Trump finally endorsed the "15 Days to Slow the Spread" guidelines produced by his CDCs, finally acknowledged the seriousness of the threat, and conceded that it was not, in fact, "a hoax."

~ ~ ~

It did not have to be this way.

In fact, with any somewhat normally functioning adult – someone chosen at random from a convenience store checkout queue, say, or a subway car – anyone willing to listen to basic facts and make reasonable decisions based on those facts, things could have been dramatically different.

If the president had bothered to take his intelligence reports seriously in the first days of January, the United States could have prepared for the arrival of the virus rather than just belatedly react to it. The production of face masks, surgical gowns and gloves could have been ramped up immediately. Hospitals could have been warned to prepare for a flood of respiratory cases. Even more important, a functioning test could have been developed and mass produced, allowing early cases to be found and isolated. Their contacts could have been traced and monitored. Most important of all, the public could have been put on guard early and enlisted in a national effort to contain the disease to the handful of cities where it had made its first appearance.

These are not hypothetical steps. They were taken by other countries: South Korea and Germany, for example. The South Korean model was probably not replicable here. The MERS outbreak there in 2015 had given its government valuable recent experience, and the coronavirus cases were largely confined to a particular religious community, making them easier to isolate. On the other hand, there was no reason that the United States could not have had an experience similar to Germany's. There, as of late August 2020, 111 people per million had died compared to 547 per million in the United States.

What's more, it was not as if the necessary expertise to do these things did not reside in our country. It did. On February 4, 2020, Jeremy Konyndyk, who worked on the Obama administration's widely praised Ebola response in 2014, wrote in the *Washington Post* that the time to prepare for a possible pandemic was now. A week earlier, on January 28, Scott Gottleib, Trump's former head of the Food and Drug Administration, wrote a similar piece with nearly identical recommendations for the *Wall Street Journal*. Tom Bossert, Trump's former homeland security adviser, was sounding those same alarms to anyone who would listen.

That universe of listeners, however, did not include the one person who mattered most: the occupant of the Oval Office.

To the contrary, Trump made it clear that he was not remotely interested in the virus, and was absolutely opposed to taking any steps that could hurt the stock market or the economy. For three years he had rebranded the steadily growing economy that Obama had left him as *the best economy in the history of the world* and was certain that it would carry him to a second term. Acknowledging that there was a genuine danger in this disease risked spooking investors, and therefore stock prices and, in his mind, hurting his chances for a second term.

This real-time aversion to the facts came atop the underlying damage Trump had already done to the nation's pandemic response infrastructure that had been built up by his predecessors, George W. Bush and Barack Obama.

Bush in his second term, having dealt with a bird-flu scare, said one of his biggest fears was a pandemic that the world simply was not prepared for. Obama, dealing with the financial crisis as he took office in January 2009, was immediately hit with the H1N1 swine flu that spring. In his second term was a major Ebola outbreak in West Africa, which he responded to by sending help to the affected areas to contain the disease there. The lessons learned in that crisis led him to institutionalize the response protocol, so it would not have to be re-invented the next time. A pandemic coordinator was added to the National Security Council, overseeing a team that resided within the various federal agencies, from Health and Human Services to the United States Agency for International Development. Officials put together a "playbook" detailing the steps to take in the event of a pandemic. During the transition to the Trump administration, Obama's public health officials even staged a "table-top" pandemic exercise for their incoming counterparts.

Trump and his people had no use for any of this. Under Trump's third national security adviser, John Bolton, he eliminated the pandemic response position from the NSC, thereby degrading the profile and efficacy of the entire team. And during 2018 and 2019, Trump eliminated two-thirds of the Beijing-based CDC officials whose job it was specifically to monitor for potential outbreaks in China. And when the coronavirus began its spread, Trump and his top aides ignored the pandemic playbook as well as the lessons from the transition training session.

The rationale behind most of these decisions was simple: If Obama did it, it must be bad. That was the foundational principle to Trump's rise within the GOP, and he continued living it in the White House, from climate change to trade to Iran to, as it turns out, our ability to cope with a deadly pandemic.

~ ~ ~

The wholesale trashing of previously acquired knowledge and expertise was bad enough, but the Trump team then compounded that with additional failures. Choosing not to ramp up the production of protective gear or to alert hospitals was a function of Trump's message that the virus was nothing to fear. But the deadliest mistake of all was likely the CDC's failure to adopt a functioning coronavirus test when it became available in late January, and its insistence instead on developing its own. When that process was badly bungled, the result was a crucial, one-month delay before a test was in widespread use across the country.

Why this happened remains unexplained. German researchers made the protocol for a working test available to the world on January 16. That became the test the World Health Organization began giving to countries without the medical infrastructure to produce their own. Trump administration

188

officials, though, refused to use that test, even as an interim measure, and pushed ahead to develop one independently. It is true the CDC has long been proud of its reputation as the world leader in public health, and perhaps the decision to wait for its own test was merely a function of that institutional pride. At the same time, Trump's simmering feud and irritation with German Chancellor Angela Merkel and his overarching "America First" rhetoric was obviously well known at the agency, and certainly within its top ranks of political appointees. Their reluctance to explain a decision to go with a German test to their boss at the White House may well explain their choice to accept a short delay.

As it turned out, unfortunately, the delay was not short. The original CDC test, shipped out three weeks after the German protocol was published but hyped as more precise because it tested for three pieces of the virus's genetic code, rather than the German test's two, contained a fatal flawed. The component of the test for that third piece of code was repeatedly producing erroneous results. Finally, nearly a month later, the CDC announced a fix: ignore that third component, and just go with the other two – meaning the Trump administration's America First test wound up no more precise than the one the rest of the world had been using for five weeks.

The consequences of this delay were nothing short of catastrophic. Had public officials been able to test for the virus widely across the country in late January, they would have been able to isolate those places where "community spread" was already taking place and acted accordingly. Elder care facilities, where nearly half of all the coronavirus fatalities have come from, could have been locked down early. Quarantines of individuals exposed to those infected might have been possible, with adequate and early testing.

But through most of the month of February, our country had none of that. Our public health officials were flying blind. Anthony Fauci, head of the infectious disease program at the National Institutes of Health, conceded afterward that not taking the German test was a mistake. "If you look back and

Monday morning quarterback it would have been nice to have had a backup," he told CNN in March.

By the time our own test was widely available, the damage was done. The virus had spread from New York and Seattle and Los Angeles, those cities where the early cases had started, all over the country. It was too late to isolate individual cases and trace their contacts. Too many people were already infected. The only recourse left was to mandate large-scale stay-at-home orders in order to slow the spread of the disease and prevent the pandemic from overwhelming all of the nation's hospitals at once.

~ ~ ~

Where America wound up by late summer, with 180,000 dead and millions sickened, was not a pre-determined outcome. Again, things did not have to go this way. They did not go this way in Germany. Indeed, had Trump handled the outbreak the way Merkel did, some hundred and fifty thousand who have died from the disease would be alive right now.

More of interest to Trump and a significant chunk of his supporters is that having effectively dealt with the virus would have also allowed the country to minimize the damage to the economy. Had it been contained in a few major cities, the rest of the nation could have largely gone about its business. We would not have needed to endure double-digit unemployment and a deep hit to gross domestic product, all while adding several trillions to the national debt.

But that economic pain – which will continue, by the way, for years to come – was a direct and predictable result of Trump's spending a full month ignoring the virus entirely, and then seven additional weeks pretending it was not really serious or that his actions had prevented it from coming into the country.

This incompetence bordering on criminal malfeasance continued largely apace after a brief pause in the days following that March 16 news conference. Trump's insecurities and

190

vanities turned what should have been a daily briefing by experts into a two-hour monologue cum political rally cum therapy session, starring himself. It was from there that he pushed his public health experts to embrace a malaria drug as a coronavirus cure. It was from there he elevated son-in-law Jared Kushner, fresh off a failed mission to deliver Middle East peace, to run the White House coronavirus response. And it was from there where he riffed on his various medical theories, including, most famously, about injecting disinfectants and bringing "very powerful light" into the body as possible cures.

The practical effect of this nonsense was that there was no national leadership at all. Whether you and your family lived or died from this disease had far more to do with the governor your state happened to have elected, and how much that particular person needed Donald Trump's support going forward. With a few exceptions – Idaho, Ohio, for example – this meant that Republican-led states were far less likely to have adopted meaningful stay-at-home directives early on, when they would have done the most good.

Trump himself, meanwhile, quickly grew bored of the pandemic, particularly after his advisers eventually persuaded him that his marathon news conferences were the cause of his slipping poll numbers. Trump had believed that his daily on-camera performances were giving him a huge advantage over Democrat Joe Biden, and frequently cited the ratings they were getting. But Americans, after initially rallying around their president, as they are wont to do in a crisis, began bailing on him as his inanity became obvious.

So it was that by late April, Trump essentially declared victory over the disease and decided to move on. The White House coronavirus task force ended its daily meetings. Top aides, following his cue, switched their focus to "re-opening" the economy and talking up favorable employment and retail sales statistics. Trump personally insisted on resuming the only part of politics or the presidency that appeared to give him any real joy, his campaign rallies. Even as Oklahoma's coronavirus numbers increased, Trump scheduled a rally in Tulsa for mid-June.

In terms of political strategy, the location was mystifying. The state's voters had favored him over Clinton by 36 points in 2016. It was nearly completely surrounded by equally Republican states. It didn't matter. The campaign and Trump himself bragged about receiving over a million requests for tickets to a 19,000-seat venue, only to have just 6,200 turn up.

In a telling Fox Business interview just days later, Trump claimed the virus would "just disappear" and that the economy would soon take off and recover all the jobs it had lost – language nearly identical to what he was saying about the pandemic in March and April.

More broadly, his message was simple : The virus was the fault of China, Obama, Biden, Democratic governors and mayors, the news media, Nancy Pelosi, anyone and everyone other than him, who, the way he told it, had done everything correctly even when facing naysayers, and whose actions prevented millions of American deaths, perhaps even "billions," as he once claimed. And by mid-June, with less than five months to go before election day, coronavirus was officially somebody else's problem. He was done with it.

As Maryland's Republican governor, Larry Hogan, described it in a mid-July *Washington Post* op-ed, Trump's failure to lead left every state on its own. "It was clear that waiting around for the president to run the nation's response was hopeless," Hogan wrote. "If we delayed any longer, we'd be condemning more of our citizens to suffering and death. So every governor went their own way, which is how the United States ended up with such a patchwork response."

~ ~ ~

When the virus has finally receded, as eventually it will, perhaps it will leave behind a chastened electorate.

Back in 2015 and 2016, one of the most common things I heard from Trump supporters was that he would shake things up. They didn't care that he had no experience in government or in running a large organization – in fact, this lack of experience was a tremendous attribute. They wanted him to be the bull in the china shop. They wanted him to overturn tables and break things.

Well, they got what they wanted, and all the rest of us have to live with the mess.

As it turns out, there are real-world consequences to mocking and driving off expertise. Oil and gas companies, pipeline companies, industries of all sorts, and Republicans generally, in fact, loved that Trump ignored the scientific consensus on climate change to make it easier for them to make money. What they didn't anticipate, perhaps, was that his disdain of science went well beyond areas where it stood to benefit them personally.

Trump offered as clear a warning as can be imagined when he took his Sharpie to that hurricane forecast map. He had no respect for trained meteorologists who had spent years and years studying tropical revolving cyclones – in his view, his judgement about the hurricane's likely path was just as valid as theirs.

So it was with the pandemic. He was fine with eliminating the Obama-era response measures because if Obama had done them, they were, by definition, bad. As to subsequent warnings by his own public health officials about the threats posed by a pandemic … well, what did experts really know, anyway? Since he never takes anything seriously until it directly threatens him, he was not at all concerned when his administration failed to rebuild the national medical supplies stockpile. He didn't pay attention when reports started circulating about a new disease in China. He didn't bother taking intelligence briefings that specifically warned him of the virus's unique dangers. In short, he failed to do any of the basic things that any even half-way competent leader would have and should have done.

This is what the know-nothings inflicted upon us all when they supported a man who was both profoundly ignorant yet proudly opinionated. The rationale behind this was that only such a person would be able to *take on the establishment* and *return power to the people.*

Burn it all down, they said, and then cheered Trump on as he did so, and put all of our lives at risk.

~ ~ ~

This rage against the system is understandable, on some level. People see economic inequality and social injustice and the simple answer is that it's all corrupt, that it truly is all rigged. Indeed, if there's any single factor explaining Trump's success with a segment of voters who supported Obama previously, it's the persistence of these ideas.

It's such an easy charge to toss out, if you're a politician running to "shake things" up. People who spend a normal amount of time thinking about politics – which is to say, very little – are receptive to this message, and those who don't pay attention to politics at all are downright hungry for it. Trump sensed this and played on it, claiming, amazingly, that only he could end the corruption because he had so often taken advantage of it in years past. That by giving campaign contributions to politicians over all those years, he had bought their loyalty for the day he needed a favor.

This argument, in fact, meshed perfectly with the message that Bernie Sanders had been selling to Democratic voters. The political system was stacked against them, and the average American had no voice.

It was an effective message, for both Sanders and Trump. It also happened to be false.

While it is true that there is occasionally corruption at all levels of government, there is nowhere near the systemic rot that so many Americans seem to want to believe exists. Maybe this is a function of better access to campaign-finance data – it is now easier than ever to determine how much campaign money Politician X has received from Special Interest Y, and journalists as well as opposing candidates are quick to draw a connection from a particular vote to a particular set of campaign contributions.

What most Americans don't realize is just how many competing interests there are, and just how expensive even House races have become. A typical re-election campaign can run several million dollars. A contested race in a competitive district can run over ten million. Are there people who honestly believe that bundled donations of $10,000 or even $50,000 is going to put a member of Congress in the back pocket of any given interest group? If you had to raise $1,000 for a charity event, are you going to be forever beholden to someone who gives you $10?

It is true that being a longtime fundraiser or a prodigious "bundler" gets your calls answered, often by the members' chiefs of staff or even the members themselves. What is not true is that those answered calls always get the desired action.

Because here is the dirty little secret behind the Washington influence game that those with a vested interest – the registered lobbyists – don't want anyone to know: Angry constituents are already the most feared group on Capitol Hill.

The Bernie Bros and the conspiracy theorists don't want to believe it's true, because it takes away all manner of excuses rooted basically in apathy or laziness. But all you have to do is watch how closely a member of Congress monitors phone calls and emails logged in the Washington and district offices. Individual notes and unscripted calls are weighted more heavily, but every contact from the district is recorded and tallied. If there are enough of them to indicate that voters back home feel strongly about any given issue, that almost always outweighs the desire of a "special interest" asking for a contrary position.

Granted, most issues are not going to generate much or perhaps even any interest from the typical voter. Most issues Congress deals with – other than ceremonial things like naming post offices – are about one business interest trying to tweak rules to gain a small advantage over a competing business interest or to obtain some public benefit at less than market cost.

And most voters are quite understandably uninterested in those skirmishes.

It's in situations like those that lawmakers are most likely to side with that lobbyist who has been the prodigious fundraiser or the loyal campaign contributor. Yet in those cases where the prodigious fundraiser or loyal contributor is asking for a vote on something that a vocal group back home opposes, the answer from the member or the chief of staff is almost always: "Sorry, I can't help you on this one."

A perfect example of the limits of campaign contributions is abortion. Notwithstanding the claims from the most committed activists on both sides – and setting aside the paychecks many of these activists derive from their activism – abortion is not "big business" for anyone involved. Performing abortions, or referring patients to doctors and clinics who perform them, is not really a profit center. Nor are "crisis pregnancy centers" or adoption agencies.

Despite this, there is hardly a more contentious issue or one that sees more grassroots lobbying. If the model of Congress as a completely corrupt entity serving only the business elites was correct, abortion would get virtually no attention from lawmakers at all.

Yet it does. That should tell us something.

On top of that, the converse is also often true. Well connected people who want something and try to use their connections frequently get squat for their efforts. Exhibit A for this could well be one Donald J. Trump, who for years in Florida paid one of Tallahassee's top lobbyists tens of thousands of dollars per year to get the state government to permit him to open a casino. The idea never moved an inch, despite the lobbying, despite all of Trump's campaign contributions to Florida Republicans. They were happy to take his money, but casino gambling was not a popular idea in Florida, and they weren't about to use even an ounce of capital just to please Trump.

~ ~ ~

In other words, and unsurprisingly, Trump lied about his ability to get politicians to do "whatever the hell you want them to do," as he famously told the *Wall Street Journal* back in the summer of 2015, a claim he repeated days later in that first Republican debate.

But that has been part and parcel of his entire con in politics. His campaign adopted the slogan "Drain the Swamp," but Trump has done no such thing. He has openly funneled millions of both taxpayer and campaign dollars into his own pocket. He has put his daughter and son-in-law in unprecedented positions of power. He and his staff routinely campaign from White House grounds and during "official" visits around the country, using government resources.

He is, hands down, the most openly corrupt president in a century, and quite possibly since the founding. And the way he tries to hide that corruption? By claiming that this is normal, that everyone is just as corrupt and just as dishonest as he is.

More important, it is also how he hides the trait that, in the end, has proven fatal to so many Americans: his fundamental incompetence and lack of judgement. Trump failed to take the basic, obvious steps than any rational adult – and even most rational children – would have taken in his position. That's the main point about being president. You don't have to be a renowned meteorologist or macroeconomist or epidemiologist. You just have to listen to them and base your decisions on their advice when the time comes.

Trump has failed to do that, time after time in any number of areas, but most consequentially for most Americans in his handling of the coronavirus pandemic. And while in some cases his failures have been due to his lack of interest, in the instance of the pandemic, it was because taking the appropriate actions would have gone against his personal interest, which was to maintain the economy and stock market through November 3 to assure himself a second term. That was the reason he didn't want to upset China's dictator, whom he was relying upon to buy more farm products to undo the effects of Trump's own trade war. It was also the reason he didn't aggressively push coronavirus testing early on. To do so would have uncovered more cases, which would have spooked consumers and investors alike.

Astonishingly, Trump even admitted all this at his fiasco of a rally in Tulsa: "When you do testing to that extent you're going to find more people, you're going to find cases. So I said to my people, 'Slow the testing down, please.'"

His staff later said he was only joking. Almost two hundred thousand dead Americans, and counting, say otherwise.

~ ~ ~

Any other politician – scratch that; any other human being would have seen the pandemic as both a responsibility and an opportunity.

As president, it is literally your job to lead the country through something like this, whether you want to or not. Americans were expecting this, and hoping Trump would rise to the occasion. That is the reason his approval ratings initially went up – not because people thought he had done a good job to that point, but because they wanted him, and the country, to do well and be safe.

Trump, naturally, drew exactly the wrong lessons from that polling bump, attributing it instead to his marathon "news conferences" he had been staging from the White House briefing room in lieu of the rallies that he could no longer hold. And, naturally, the more he talked, the more average Americans realized just how ignorant and dangerous he truly was, peaking with that famous April 23 medical advice to inject disinfectants into the lungs and get ultraviolet or "very powerful light" into the body. Somehow.

The great irony is that had Trump been capable of leading, and had done even a halfway competent job, he could have cruised to re-election as the nation's savior, without ever leaving the White House. It could have been a straightforward

198

Rose Garden strategy, with minimal campaigning, leading to another four years.

It's what any of the other candidates running in 2016, in either party, would have done. It's what any normal, adult human being would have done.

That Trump was unwilling and unable even to try tells Americans everything they need to know.

11. Republican Requiem

B ack in that parallel universe where then-GOP chairman Reince Priebus and the rest of the party establishment have smacked down Donald Trump in the infancy of his campaign and the normal laws of politics have reasserted themselves, the present-day timeline sees President Jeb Bush, having successfully contained the pandemic in early spring, signing the biggest immigration reform package in a generation. It makes the "dreamer" cohort – those who were brought into the country illegally as children – eligible for immediate naturalization. It revises the criteria for green cards. And it grants amnesty for everyone in the country illegally and allows for citizenship after a decade.

His signature on the bill is the last straw for the nativist wing of the Republican Party. The Breitbartians and Stephen Millers and Stephen Bannons vow to back a third-party candidate in 2020, but to no practical effect. Indeed, Jeb winds up winning 55 percent of the Latino vote nationally in his re-election, more than making up for the loss of the single-issue racists and xenophobes who hate him for failing to keep brown people out of the country.

And that statistic truly becomes the most significant thing to come out of the third Bush presidency, imposing upon his party a radical change in direction that allows for a sustainable future. By giving real-life implementation to the key recommendations of that 2013 "autopsy," the Republican Party again becomes a national force as the center-right balance to the Democrats.

In our own, actual universe, of course, all of that is fantasy.

Here, the Republican establishment knowingly elected an unscrupulous con artist who played to single-issue racists and xenophobes to win the nomination. And then it stuck with him after he became president, despite increasingly erratic behavior that made the childish insults and buffoonery during his campaign seem downright normal in contrast.

Trump, unsurprisingly, has shown almost zero effort or interest in reaching out to anyone beyond his hardcore base of white nationalists and cultural reactionaries. Meaning that the future of the Republican Party remains hostage to a game show host-turned president at least through this election – and maybe years more, should he win.

The difference for the party of Lincoln between those possible outcomes cannot be overstated.

~ ~ ~

Shakespeare wrote in *Julius Caesar*: "The fault, dear Brutus, is not in our stars, but in ourselves."

And so it is with today's Republican Party. Their root problem, as it turns out, was not really with their national leaders in recent elections, but with their base. Because, as it also turns out, Hillary Clinton was right.

On September 10, 2016, speaking to donors at a New York City fundraiser, Clinton offered her take on who, exactly, was supporting Donald Trump, a man so despised by such a wide variety of people that many seemed genuinely curious as to what sort of person did *not* despise him. She explained that there were some people who simply could not get past their various bigotries, and that she would never be able to reach them.

"You know, to just be grossly generalistic, you could put half of Trump's supporters into what I call the basket of deplorables. Right? The racist, sexist, homophobic, xenophobic, Islamaphobic — you name it. And unfortunately there are people like that. And he has lifted them up."

She was pilloried for that assessment by, naturally, Trump's campaign and the Republican Party, who immediately misrepresented what she had said, claiming that she had labeled *all* Trump voters as racist or misogynist or so on. She was also pounded by political analysts in the media, particularly on cable television for her terrible "gaffe" and how it proved yet again her tin ear and inability to connect with ordinary Americans.

Let's accept for a moment that opining on the motives of your opponent's supporters in the heat of a political campaign is never going to end well. Barack Obama caught all manner of grief for his "bitter clingers" remark back in 2008. Mitt Romney's "47 percent" analysis may have made it impossible for him to win in 2012. Elections are about adding to your coalition, not subtracting, and Clinton and everyone else should know by now that in this age, there are probably more recording devices in your audience than there are people. On top of that, we can also accept that she was not a great candidate, in terms of the performance artistry that has come to require.

But what got lost in the critique of her statement's politics, though, was a reckoning of its accuracy. Especially with the hindsight of having three and a half years of Trump's record and the knowledge of what sorts of people truly support his words and deeds, it comes to this: In what way was she wrong?

At low points of his presidency, his declaring a "national emergency" over his failure to win congressional funding for a border wall to keep out Latino immigrants, say, or his response to Charlottesville, when America got a good, unvarnished glimpse of the real Donald Trump, what sorts of people were still defending his behavior? As it turns out, it was those who feel threatened by the America of today and even more by the America of tomorrow. Those who feel "their" nation would be a better place if these others with the different colored skin or different gods were not in it. Those whose idea of Christianity is more about excluding all the "others" than it is about the power of grace. In other words: those driven primarily by racism, sexism, homophobia, xenophobia. You name it.

Of course, even back in 2016, it wasn't a big secret what sorts of people were drawn to Donald Trump, particularly in the Republican primaries. What did people think his supporters were talking about when they said they loved that he was "not politically correct" and that he "said what everyone was thinking"? To many, many base Republican voters, political correctness meant not being able to call Black people niggers, gay people faggots or to tell women to shut the hell up.

And four years into Trump's efforts to reshape the party he hijacked to reflect the values of his core supporters, this has become the intractable problem underlying the Republican Party's woes. Their hardcore primary voters truly are deplorable.

And yes, the Republican Party *has* catered to deplorables – fairly openly back in 1968, less openly since then, until Trump came along and happily and loudly anointed himself King of the Deplorables.

~ ~ ~

I will concede that not only did I not see Trump coming, I flat out refused to see him coming.

One autumn day in 2015, a colleague of mine at *National Journal*, someone who had been covering national politics far longer than I, came over to my desk and said he was worried about the dark tone of the Trump rallies, with the hate and the anger right out in the open and the authoritarianism just under the surface. He worried that Trump had zero knowledge or interest in democracy, and that should he win, it would mean dangerous times for the country.

I was so irritated I practically shouted at him. Donald Trump is not going to win the Republican nomination, let alone become president of the United States, I declared. I knew this for certain because I had faith in the strength of political parties. I had seen over the years that, in the end, the party decides. I had watched John McCain's rebellion in 2000 get squashed like an insect by the Bush machine after his big New Hampshire upset. Four years later, the institutional Democratic Party chose with its head rather than its heart, quickly settling on John Kerry over Howard Dean as the best bet to unseat Bush. How would

Trump possibly survive when the Republican Party decided that play time was over?

I owe that colleague an apology. Just as I owe an apology to my *HuffPost* colleague who, some nine months later, was the sole person in the newsroom meeting to raise her hand and suggest that Trump would win the election because, in her view, people were not fully appreciating the underlying racism and sexism in our culture. I had rolled my eyes, and was among the plurality in the room who believed that Hillary Clinton would not only win, but win with a larger Electoral College margin than Barack Obama had won in 2008.

True, I didn't appreciate then the extent of Russian efforts to help Trump, and I couldn't know that James Comey would weigh in in the closing days as he did. Yet even with those factors, a candidate as proudly and dangerously ignorant and as openly racist as Donald Trump, I would have thought, could not have broken 40 percent all these decades after the Civil Rights Act.

I had thought the last gasp of the reactionaries was doomed to the march of progress, that Barack Obama's re-election in particular had proven that.

I was wrong, and naively so.

~ ~ ~

Part of that naiveté, perhaps, comes from being old enough to remember how much worse things used to be, to appreciate how much things have changed even in my lifetime.

As late as the early 1990s, I was astounded to hear the "N" word coming from the lips of white people in Central Florida – college-educated, reasonably-well-off white people. A NASA employee. The adult daughter of a respected local judge. They were not trying to be scandalous. That is how they still talked when there were no Black people around to hear them.

Still, attitudes then were a marked change from attitudes three decades earlier, when the majority of white people would have been fine using that word even in the presence of Black people. Similarly, norms now are markedly different from what they were at the start of the final decade of the last century, at a time when it was still inconceivable that America could elect a Black president in the foreseeable future.

And these new societal norms, in fact, are the "political correctness" that so many Trump supporters say they are so sick of. While conservative media obsess over the silly nomenclature fights on college campuses, what a significant percentage of real Trump voters in the real world mean when they refer to "political correctness" is the generally accepted norm in society that you shouldn't use racial slurs or discriminate against people based on the color of their skin.

This is the politics of white grievance, the politics of restoration of an era where this kind of speech and behavior was perfectly acceptable. And to them, Donald Trump was the first politician in decades willing to stand up for them.

It was easy to forget how many Americans still thought that way, in a country that had celebrated the election of its first Black president just eight years earlier.

Lyndon Johnson had spoken about turning over the South to Republicans for a generation, but "South" over the decades has really come to mean much of rural and exurban America. The sorts of places where people who are still angry at the Democratic Party for completing the promise of the Civil War and the 13th and 14th amendments make up a significant plurality, if not an outright majority.

Many of these were Democrats, prior to the great realignment that has taken place in recent decades, and disproportionately so in the South. In the election of 2016, they were the "shy" Trump supporters, that slice of the populace who understood that societal norms had made racism unacceptable, and that openly supporting Trump's out-in-the-open racism would invite criticism that they would just as soon avoid.

Increased voter turnout in rural and exurban areas certainly boosts the theory that Trump was able to bring to the polls Americans who perhaps had given up on voting because no candidate, not even the Republican, was willing to talk about Black and brown people the way Trump was.

~ ~ ~

In fairness, while the overt appeal to race was an enormously important factor in Trump's ability to win a large enough plurality in the 2016 primaries to secure the Republican nomination, it was not the only factor.

It is hard to tease out, because of the large overlap of racially motivated Trump supporters who also cited it, but "economic anxiety" did play some role in Trump's success in both the GOP primaries as well as the general election.

Trump has proven through the years that he lacks the patience, the ability for strategic thinking or the discipline to run a successful business. Florida Senator Marco Rubio put it bluntly during one of the later 2016 debates, when he told Trump that had he not been born rich, he would likely be found on the streets of Manhattan scamming tourists, not in the penthouse of a high-rise. "If he hadn't inherited $200 million, you know where Donald Trump would be right now? Selling watches in Manhattan," he said.

Yet Trump is not entirely stupid, and as Rubio correctly alluded to, his gift – such as it is – is conning people. Throughout his years in his various businesses, in "reality" television and, most recently, in politics, Trump's one talent is his ability to read a room, and then through sheer bluster and noise level persuade a shockingly large percentage of the people in it to believe him.

People believed him when he told them he knew how to run casinos, and a number of big-deal bankers who should have known better were nearly ruined when he bankrupted those casinos, instead. From the platform of a primetime NBC game show dressed up as a "reality" series, Trump persuaded a huge swath of America that he was a successful and savvy multi-billionaire businessman, when his actual record suggested exactly the opposite.

Using that national name ID, Trump for years flirted with the idea of running for president, then in 2015 actually did so, promising people everything from making Mexico pay for a border wall to re-writing trade agreements to bringing millions of overseas jobs back into the United States. A great number of voters appeared to believe those claims, too.

And now, as president, Trump has taken to claiming that he has delivered on all those promises, even when he plainly has not. And, amazingly, a large percentage of Americans continue to stand by him.

Some, of course, appear not to *really* believe him about much at all, but continue to defend and support him because he is a tool – a "useful idiot" – who is at least working to bring about their true, "politically incorrect" goals.

Others appear not entirely persuaded by everything or even many of the things that he claims, but defend him anyway because they desperately want him to accomplish those things he said that he would – because *his* success would prove that *their* decision to support him against the advice of all the so-called experts was sound. And, incidentally, his success would also prove that they, personally, are not stupid.

That's really what so much of this is about, as I have seen firsthand at Trump rallies through the years. Even presented with a list of Trump's claimed accomplishments that a cursory Google search would show to be false, most Trump supporters I spoke with continued to claim that Trump was correct. Some would try to make excuses for him, saying that looking at the facts a different way would show that Trump was generally right, even if the specific instances he himself cited were wrong. Others said that even if I was correct, and Trump had not done what he was claiming, that President Obama had been much worse, and why didn't I report that? Still others refused to even look at the list of falsehoods I was asking them to review. They would push the paper away and tell me they believed Trump and that it was my word against his.

In their defense of Trump, a couple of things were noticeable right away. First, they were not remotely interested in any actual facts. Theirs was almost entirely an emotional attachment. Deep down, my sense was that they knew all five of Trump's repeated claims on my list were false, as were so many other things he says. They just didn't want anyone to ruin their fantasy of a strong leader who cared about what people like them believed and wanted.

It was more than a little pathetic. A great number of liberals see the seething anger on display at a Trump rally and fear that he is stoking a new fascism that could sweep the country. Having been to a great many of them during his 2016 campaign, and then more still in the years since, as Trump sought out the love and affirmation from his fans that pretty much no one in Washington was willing to give him, I have come to a different view.

The majority of the attendees at these shows – because that is what they are, first and foremost: entertainment extravaganzas – were not scary or demented or paranoid as much as they were sad. They longed for an America that existed primarily on TV shows of the 1950s and 60s – "Father Knows Best" or "Leave it to Beaver." An America of white families enjoying success with a birthright promise of even greater plenty in the coming generations.

Most Republican politicians understand full well that returning to that gauzy, didn't-really-happen-that-way time is never going to happen. Trump, if he understands it, doesn't care. He'll say what his loyal fans want to hear, over and over and over again. Even they know, I believe, that it's an impossible promise. They just like hearing him say it.

And there, I think, is the genuine connection between Trump and his supporters. Too often people look at Donald Trump and wonder how this Ivy League graduate with all the millionaire friends can have such a loyal following among white working class folks who typically have at best a high school diploma.

The answer is simple: While Trump aspired to be accepted by the elite, he never really was. He was too needy, too mouthy, too loud and, frankly, too big a fraud to be taken seriously by the very people whose approval he craved. There is a profound inferiority complex underlying so many of his words and actions – one that is shared by so many of those who support him.

The deep-seated anger and anxiety about the structure of the national and global economy is understandable. There is obviously enough wealth in this country and on this planet for every human being to live a dignified life, with access to food, clean water and basic medical care. That increased use of robots in our factories and farms and, soon enough, white-collar offices will end the livelihoods of millions or even tens of millions more of us in the coming decades is obviously and quite reasonably distressing.

Trump was able to take advantage of that – not because he had a realistic plan to improve their lot. Rather, because he lacks even a hint of the scruples that keeps ordinary people from promising things that they know they simply cannot deliver.

~ ~ ~

That said, it seems highly unlikely that Republicans can find someone else to replicate Trump's success. There aren't enough voters driven primarily by racism to win a national election. Trump, because of the character he played on his TV show, was able to con a substantial number of people into believing that he could end their financial worries with no additional effort required on their part – that with the snap of his fingers, he could turn economic reality on its head and turn the clock back six decades. When that fails to happen, that segment of the population that decided to take a chance on him specifically because they believed he would improve their bottom line is less likely to make that gamble on a Trump remake (Indeed, they may not even stick with the original Trump for a second term, given how badly Trump has wrecked the economy through his botched coronavirus response).

More to the point, the next open Republican primary field is almost certain *not* to have a loud, self-proclaimed genius with an easy answer for everything and with 100 percent name ID and enough money to self-fund through the primaries. Which means it will revert more to the mean, which means that the party's 2013 "autopsy" of the 2012 loss should probably be recovered from the backup disks and printed out again.

Whether it's November 3 or four years from now, the day will come when the reality of demographic change rises up and smacks Republicans in the face. In astrophysics, the old saying is that gravity always wins, after the strong and weak nuclear forces have spent themselves. Just so, gravity will win out in American electoral politics, as well.

Trump's bullhorn of racism cannot work for any other Republican – the fact is, it barely worked for him, and it wouldn't have were it not for that Comey-Putin rogue wave. And we saw from the 2012 election that the party's less overt, "don't say the quiet part at all, let alone out loud" dog whistles aren't likely to work, either.

Pandering to ethno-white-nationalists turns off more people than it brings in, a trend that is likely to get even more pronounced as ethnic minorities and people of multiple races make up an ever larger percentage of the population.

This was true in 2012, and it remains true today. Trump was a blip, an out-of-family data point.

~ ~ ~

Eventually, either this coming January or four Januaries hence, Donald Trump will be gone, and the Republican Party will be dead.

Trump has reshaped it now so thoroughly in his own image – with plenty of enthusiastic support from within the party establishment, by the way – that it will be impossible to return to "normal" anytime soon. This is what happens when an organization has no objective other than to win.

Not long after Trump's election, one long-time Republican National Committee member waxed philosophically to me that perhaps it was time for the party to evolve to a new iteration. I

210

listened in stunned silence as he explained how maybe a populist party was the way forward, building on the white, non-college-educated working class that Trump brought out and made Republican.

I asked what other groups would be in this coalition. He allowed that he hadn't quite figured out that part yet.

It is doubtful that either he or anyone else will. Trump has so thoroughly turned off pretty much every demographic group outside of white, low-education rural and exurban voters that it's hard to see how a party that slavishly defended his every offensive, ridiculous or just plain nuts remark or action can bring them back.

Trump truly was a black swan event. How many other unscrupulous, dishonest con men are out there willing to brazenly lie about their qualifications who also happen to have a near universal name recognition thanks to a popular prime-time network television show? As of this writing, that number is precisely zero. Even if there was such a person, it seems certain that Trump's rolling train wreck of a White House – culminating in more than a quarter million Americans dead from the coronavirus by Election Day – will make that style of leadership something to be avoided at all cost by a sizeable plurality, if not outright majority, of the electorate.

There's no point in hoping for Republican "elder statesmen" to come salvage the party in the near- or mid-term future. Recall that heading into November 2016, most of the "grownups" in the party wound up supporting Trump, knowing full well what that meant for the country. As another top Republican National Committee member, a veteran of previous White Houses and a good number of presidential campaigns, told me in the first chaotic months of the Trump presidency: "Our job is to win. We won."

Yes, they did. Thanks to James Comey and the Russians and a deeply disliked Democratic nominee, they won – not because of Trump, but in spite of him.

Older white people who get all their information from Fox News and Rush Limbaugh are not suddenly finding a magic fountain-of-youth elixir just because Donald Trump is president. Texas did not suddenly stop becoming ever more Latino just because Stephen Miller has concocted new and different ways to make them feel unwelcome. Younger people have not stopped reshaping southern cities like Atlanta and Charlotte and Orlando. These demographic changes are moving ahead just as they were before Donald Trump ever rode down his escalator.

The only thing that has changed is that the segments of the population that are growing – Latinos and Asians – have come to feel even more alienated from the Republican Party. For the vast majority of young people, that is Americans aged thirty and under, Trump's Republican Party has become essentially an epithet. So much so that the historically apathetic voting bloc nearly doubled its turnout rate in the 2018 midterm elections compared to four years earlier. Yes, the cohort that has had to be wooed and cajoled to exercise their constitutional right and civic duty in presidential elections came out in force to punish Trump even when he wasn't on the ballot.

There is a reason that so many Republican incumbents in suddenly uncertain districts decided to retire from the House of Representatives heading into the 2018 election. They understood that theirs was now the Party Of And For Donald Trump, and they decided that an uphill fight just to return as a member of the minority party still in his control simply was not worth it.

There is certainly the chance that once Trump is gone, the Republican Party will steer back to the course it had set in 2013. Dust off the "Growth and Opportunity Project" report. Update it a bit. Maybe add a new prologue to explain what, exactly, happened in 2016. Perhaps that will work, and longtime Republicans will be at the vanguard of the Movement To Forget Trump Ever Happened.

Perhaps. And then again, perhaps not.

California Republicans already learned the lesson of ginning up white grievance politics, way back in the mid-1990s. Proposition 187 was designed by Republicans to ride white anger over illegal Mexican immigrants back to power. Governor Pete Wilson thought he could parlay it into the 1996 presidential nomination. Instead, he and his party alienated Latino voters, who have voted Democratic in overwhelming numbers ever since.

Trump's presidency, incredibly, made the situation in the state that produced Ronald Reagan even worse. California Republicans lost another seven House seats in 2018, including those in once-upon-a-time solidly GOP Orange County. Out of 53 House seats representing the state, Republicans now hold all of eight, and that includes one it picked up in a May 2020 special election forced by the resignation of one of those newly elected Democrats in a sex scandal.

What if by the end of his tenure, Trump has spread that infection even further? What happens when Arizona and Georgia finally vote Democratic? Indeed, what happens when Texas does?

You can roll credits on the Republican Party, is what happens. There simply are not enough states where angry white people with no college degrees constitute big enough voting blocs to make up for losing those fast-growing states teeming with the "new" America.

Donald Trump will have killed a major American political party, and its members will have helped him do it nearly every step of the way.

~ ~ ~

There is a poignant moment in the movie *The Caine Mutiny* during the celebration of the acquittals when the defense lawyer who has just saved his clients' lives confronts the executive officer and demands to know if he has ever stopped to consider things from Captain Queeg's point of view. If, instead of mocking him behind his back and treating him like a pariah, they had given Queeg the respect he was owed and worked with him to smooth out the rough patches, whether maybe the whole confrontation during the typhoon might have been avoided. If

Queeg, had he known that his officers had his back, might have been more willing to take their advice when it really mattered.

I've sometimes thought about that scene, watching a hapless Donald Trump conclude – correctly – that almost nobody with any talent or judgement or leadership skills believes he is remotely qualified for the job or even much likes him personally. I wonder what might have happened if the best and the brightest had worked with him and co-opted him instead of openly resisting him from the start.

Of course, in the film, Humphrey Bogart is merely the skipper of a Navy minesweeper. In real life, Donald Trump is in charge of the entire executive branch of the United States, including, most consequentially, the most powerful armed forces in the world.

And, of course, there were a number of talented people who did attempt to treat him with great deference but who were repaid with scorn nonetheless. Defense secretary James Mattis, national security adviser H.R. McMaster, even secretary of state Rex Tillerson eventually lost influence and, when push came to shove, were unable to prevent Trump from making bad choices.

More to the point, Captain Queeg was, at his core, a good person. A damaged person, yes, at least in part as a result of trauma suffered during service to his country. Paranoid and abusive, but still fundamentally moral.

And this is where any resemblance to Donald Trump disappears. Because our president does not operate from a moral code. There is no sense of an intrinsic right and wrong and an attempt to live by that. There is only: What can I get away with? And: Do unto others before they do unto you.

This has nothing to do with ideology or politics. Liberals, conservatives, libertarians, Marxists. All can be good people. All can put the interests of the country ahead of their own personal interests. As these past three and a half years have shown quite clearly, Donald Trump cannot.

And so this is the question for Americans: What would a thoroughly amoral president completely unburdened by the prospect of having to face the electorate again do in a second term?

We've already seen that Republicans in Congress cannot be counted on to check his worst behavior, with the singular exception of Mitt Romney in the Senate. We've already seen that his Attorney General Bill Barr seems to believe that Trump has a right to be treated as a monarch, and is likely to continue to encourage his acting out.

It could well be that Trump's only ambition for a second term is to win it, to avoid that big capital "L" that America stamps onto the forehead of one-term presidents. It could be that he effectively moves to Mar-a-Lago from November through May and Bedminster for the rest of the year and spends most of his days golfing.

But what if he decides that it will be his legacy to make the country "great" and starts to use those powers at his disposal to do so? We've seen him deploy the military to the Mexican border in service of the 2018 midterm election. We've seen him declare a state of emergency to divert money for his wall when Congress would not appropriate any. We've seen him violently clear a public square of peaceful protesters so that he could go be photographed holding a Bible in front of a church. We've watched him lose interest in a deadly pandemic after concluding that taking it seriously was only hurting his chances for re-election.

How far will he go? And do we really want to find out?

Beyond him personally are his enablers, the ones who saw in him a useful idiot to get conservative judges and tax cuts and so forth while knowing full well that he was mentally and emotionally unqualified for the job. These are the ones who knew better, and who are equally responsible for those extra millions of Americans who got seriously ill and the one hundred and fifty thousand, at least, who have needlessly died because of Trump's incompetence.

If Trump were to win again, there is a good chance that Mitch McConnell and the Christian Right and the Republican

National Committee will believe it was all somehow worth it, in the end.

Americans will have to decide if that's the lesson they want to give them.

Sources

I am indebted to my many colleagues at the White House who have teased out detail upon detail about the dysfunction in that building these past three and a half years. That body of work has added context to the president's many utterances and social media statements, without which this book would not have been possible. I am also grateful to the reporting of the president and his policies by colleagues not on the White House beat, particularly those who have broken major stories on intelligence, national security and immigration. It has been phenomenal and a true public service.

Most of the facts in the narrative are from my own observations and reporting and from confirming work first published elsewhere. I have cited significant work that I relied upon below, and in some cases in the body of the text, as well.

1. The Useful Idiot

Bolton, John R. The Room Where It Happened: A White House Memoir. Kindle edition, Simon and Schuster, 2020.

Fahrenthold, David A. "Trump agrees to shut down his charity amid allegations that he used it for personal and political benefit." Washingtonpost.com, Dec. 18, 2018, https://www.washingtonpost.com/politics/trump-agrees-to-shut-down-his-charity-amid-allegations-he-used-it-for-personal-and-political-

benefit/2018/12/18/dd3f5030-021b-11e9-9122-
82e98f91ee6f_story.html. Accessed Aug. 1, 2020.

Harris, Shane and Greg Miller, Josh Dawsey and Ellen
Nakashima. "U.S. intelligence reports from January
and February warned about a likely pandemic."
Washingtonpost.com, March 20, 2020,
https://www.washingtonpost.com/national-security/us-
intelligence-reports-from-january-and-february-
warned-about-a-likely-
pandemic/2020/03/20/299d8cda-6ad5-11ea-b5f1-
a5a804158597_story.html. Accessed Aug. 1, 2020.

@NWSBirmingham (National Weather Service Birmingham).
"Alabama will NOT see any impacts from #Dorian.
We repeat, no impacts from Hurricane #Dorian will be
felt across Alabama. The system will remain too far
east. #alwx." Twitter, Sept. 1, 2019, 11:11 am,
https://twitter.com/NWSBirmingham/status/11681796
47667814400.

@realDonaldTrump (Donald J. Trump). "In addition to
Florida - South Carolina, North Carolina, Georgia, and
Alabama, will most likely be hit (much) harder than
anticipated. Looking like one of the largest hurricanes
ever. Already category 5. BE CAREFUL! GOD
BLESS EVERYONE!" Twitter, Sept. 1, 2019, 10:51
a.m.,
https://twitter.com/realDonaldTrump/status/116817461
3827899393.

@realDonaldTrump (Donald J. Trump). "WE CANNOT LET
THE CURE BE WORSE THAN THE PROBLEM
ITSELF. AT THE END OF THE 15 DAY PERIOD,
WE WILL MAKE A DECISION AS TO WHICH
WAY WE WANT TO GO!" Twitter, March 22, 2020,
11:50 p.m.,
https://twitter.com/realDonaldTrump/status/124193528
5916782593.

Rothfeld, Michael and Alexandra Berzon. "Donald Trump and the Mob: His real-estate developments in Atlantic City and New York brought the GOP nominee into regular contact with people who had ties to organized crime; he says he's 'the cleanest guy there is.'" Wsj.com, Sept. 1, 2016, https://www.wsj.com/articles/donald-trump-dealt-with-a-series-of-people-who-had-mob-ties-1472736922. Accessed Aug. 1, 2020.

2. The Rogue Wave

BBC staff. "Vladimir Putin: Russia's action man president." BBC.com, July 2, 2020, https://www.bbc.com/news/world-europe-15047823. Accessed Aug. 2, 2020.

3. A Creature of the Tabloids

Bush, Billy. "Billy Bush: Yes, Donald Trump, You Said That." Nytimes.com, Dec. 3, 2017, https://www.nytimes.com/2017/12/03/opinion/billy-bush-trump-access-hollywood-tape.html. Accessed Aug. 4, 2020.

Carswell, Sue. "Trump Says Goodbye Marla, Hello Carla." People.com, July 8, 1991, https://people.com/archive/trump-says-goodbye-marla-hello-carla-vol-35-no-26/. Accessed Aug. 4, 2020.

Dáte, S.V. "The 1 Easy Way Donald Trump Could Have Been Even Richer: Doing Nothing." Nationaljournal.com, Aug. 26, 2015, https://www.nationaljournal.com/s/54699/1-easy-way-donald-trump-could-have-been-even-richer-doing-nothing. Accessed Aug. 4, 2020.

Johnston, David Cay. The Making of Donald Trump. Kindle edition, Penguin, 2016.

Keefe, Patrick Radden. "How Mark Burnett Resurrected Donald Trump as an Icon of American Success." Newyorker.com, Dec. 27, 2018, https://www.newyorker.com/magazine/2019/01/07/how-mark-burnett-resurrected-donald-trump-as-an-icon-of-american-success. Accessed Aug. 4, 2020.

Mayer, Jane. "Donald Trump's Ghostwriter Tells All." Newyorker.com, July 18, 2016, https://www.newyorker.com/magazine/2016/07/25/donald-trumps-ghostwriter-tells-all. Accessed Aug. 4, 2020.

McCammond, Alexi and Jonathan Swan. "Scoop: Insider leaks Trump's 'Executive Time'-filled private schedules." Axios.com, Feb. 3, 2019, https://www.axios.com/donald-trump-private-schedules-leak-executive-time-34e67fbb-3af6-48df-aefb-52e02c334255.html. Accessed Aug. 4, 2020.

4. Nixon's Deal with the Devil

Dáte, S.V. "In Race To Replace Cantor, Southern Republicans See Opportunity." NPR.org, June 18, 2014, https://www.npr.org/2014/06/18/323351113/in-race-to-replace-cantor-southern-republicans-see-opportunity. Accessed Aug. 4, 2020.

Dáte, S.V. "Way Back Pre-Trump, Republicans Actually Wanted To Do Better With Minorities: The president's courting of disaffected white voters could be painting his party into a demographic corner." Huffpost.com, Aug. 28, 2017, https://www.huffpost.com/entry/trump-republican-party-

minorities_n_59a0a7c7e4b06d67e337af62. Accessed
Aug. 4, 2020.

Hensch, Mark. "Rubio: Obama has 'deliberately weakened
America.'" Thehill.com, Jan. 4, 2016,
https://thehill.com/blogs/ballot-box/presidential-
races/264627-rubio-obama-has-deliberately-weakened-
america. Accessed Aug. 4, 2020.

Mooney, Alexander. "Trump sends investigators to Hawaii to
look into Obama." CNN.com, April 7, 2011,
https://politicalticker.blogs.cnn.com/2011/04/07/trump
-sends-investigators-to-hawaii-to-look-into-obama/.
Accessed Aug. 4, 2020.

Republican National Committee. "Growth and Opportunity
Project." Documentcloud.org, March 18, 2013,
https://assets.documentcloud.org/documents/623752/rn
c-report-growth-opportunity-book-2013.pdf. Accessed
Aug. 4, 2020.

5. The Stephens Find Their Stooge

Allen, Mike. "RNC Chief to Say It Was 'Wrong' to Exploit
Racial Conflict for Votes." Washingtonpost.com, July
14, 2005,
https://www.washingtonpost.com/archive/politics/2005
/07/14/rnc-chief-to-say-it-was-wrong-to-exploit-racial-
conflict-for-votes/66889840-8d59-44e1-8784-
5c9b9ae85499/. Accessed Aug. 5, 2020.

Glosser, David S. "Stephen Miller Is an Immigration
Hypocrite. I Know Because I'm His Uncle: If my
nephew's ideas on immigration had been in force a
century ago, our family would have been wiped out."
Politico.com, Aug. 13, 2018,
https://www.politico.com/magazine/story/2018/08/13/s

tephen-miller-is-an-immigration-hypocrite-i-know-because-im-his-uncle-219351. Accessed Aug. 5, 2020.

Green, Joshua. "This Man Is the Most Dangerous Political Operative in America: Steve Bannon runs the new vast right-wing conspiracy—and he wants to take down both Hillary Clinton and Jeb Bush." Bloomberg.com, Oct. 8, 2015, https://www.bloomberg.com/politics/graphics/2015-steve-bannon/. Accessed Aug. 5, 2020.

Hayden, Michael Edison. "Stephen Miller's Affinity for White Nationalism Revealed in Leaked Emails." Splcenter.org, Nov. 12, 2019, https://www.splcenter.org/hatewatch/2019/11/12/stephen-millers-affinity-white-nationalism-revealed-leaked-emails. Accessed Aug. 5, 2020.

Ioffe, Julia. "The Believer: How Stephen Miller went from obscure Capitol Hill staffer to Donald Trump's warm-up act—and resident ideologue." Politico.com, June 27, 2016, https://www.politico.com/magazine/story/2016/06/stephen-miller-donald-trump-2016-policy-adviser-jeff-sessions-213992. Accessed Aug. 5, 2020.

Kessler, Ronald. "Donald Trump: Mean-Spirited GOP Won't Win Elections." Newsmax.com, Nov. 26, 2012, https://www.newsmax.com/Newsfront/Donald-Trump-Ronald-Kessler/2012/11/26/id/465363/. Accessed Aug. 5, 2020.

Moody, Chris. "The Time I Went To Summer Camp with the Future Mini-Trump." cnn.com, April 2017, https://www.cnn.com/interactive/2017/politics/state/the-time-i-went-to-summer-camp-with-the-future-mini-trump/. Accessed Aug. 5, 2020.

Perlstein, Rick. "Exclusive -- Lee Atwater's Infamous 1981 Interview on the Southern Strategy: The forty-two-minute recording, acquired by James Carter IV,

222

confirms Atwater's incendiary remarks and places them in context." Thenation.com, Nov. 13, 2012, https://www.thenation.com/article/archive/exclusive-lee-atwaters-infamous-1981-interview-southern-strategy/. Accessed Aug. 5, 2020.

Ryan, Patrick. "Ava DuVernay lets Trump 'speak for himself' in Central Park Five series 'When They See Us.'" USAToday.com, June 6, 2019, https://www.usatoday.com/story/life/tv/2019/06/03/loo king-back-trumps-involvement-1989-central-park-five-case/1212335001/. Accessed Aug. 5, 2020.

Shear, Michael D. and Julie Hirschfeld Davis. "Stoking Fear, Trump Defied Bureaucracy to Advance Immigration Agenda." Nytimes.com, Dec. 23, 2017, https://www.nytimes.com/2017/12/23/us/politics/trum p-immigration.html?_r=1. Accessed Aug. 5, 2020.

Dawsey, Josh. "Trump derides protections for immigrants from 'shithole' countries." Washingtonpost.com, Jan. 12, 2018, https://www.washingtonpost.com/politics/trump-attacks-protections-for-immigrants-from-shithole-countries-in-oval-office-meeting/2018/01/11/bfc0725c-f711-11e7-91af-31ac729add94_story.html?wpisrc=al_news__alert-politics--alert-national&wpmk=1. Accessed Aug. 5, 2020.

6. The Party of Lincoln Becomes the Party of Trump

Flegenheimer, Matt. "Stephen Miller, the Powerful Survivor on the President's Right Flank: Mr. Miller, who was a conservative trapped in a liberal California high school, has rocketed to the upper reaches of White House influence, especially on immigration."

Nytimes.com, Oct. 9, 2017,
https://www.nytimes.com/2017/10/09/us/politics/steph
en-miller-trump-white-house.html. Accessed Aug. 5,
2020.

Green, Joshua. "This Man Is the Most Dangerous Political
Operative in America: Steve Bannon runs the new vast
right-wing conspiracy—and he wants to take down
both Hillary Clinton and Jeb Bush." Bloomberg.com,
Oct. 8, 2015,
https://www.bloomberg.com/politics/graphics/2015-
steve-bannon/. Accessed Aug. 5, 2020.

The New York Times. "Donald Trump's New York Times
Interview: Full Transcript." Nytimes.com, Nov. 23,
2016,
https://www.nytimes.com/2016/11/23/us/politics/trum
p-new-york-times-interview-transcript.html. Accessed
Aug. 5, 2020.

Department of Homeland Security. "Joint Statement from the
Department Of Homeland Security and Office of the
Director of National Intelligence on Election Security."
Dhs.gov, Oct. 7, 2016,
https://www.dhs.gov/news/2016/10/07/joint-statement-
department-homeland-security-and-office-director-
national. Accessed Aug. 5, 2020.

Mashal, Mujib and Eric Schmitt, Najim Rahim and Rukmini
Callimachi. "Afghan Contractor Handed Out Russian
Cash to Kill Americans, Officials Say." Nytimes.com,
July 13, 2020,
https://www.nytimes.com/2020/07/01/world/asia/afgha
n-russia-bounty-middleman.html. Accessed Aug. 5,
2020.

7. God, Guns and Russia

Balmer, Randall. "The Real Origins of the Religious Right." Politico.com, May 27, 2014, https://www.politico.com/magazine/story/2014/05/rcli gious-right-real-origins-107133. Accessed Aug. 5, 2020.

Brody, David. "EXCLUSIVE White House Press Secretary Sarah Sanders: 'God Wanted Donald Trump to Become President.'" Cbn.com, Jan. 30, 2019, https://www1.cbn.com/cbnnews/politics/2019/january/ exclusive-white-house-press-secretary-sarah-sanders-god-wanted-donald-trump-to-become-president. Accessed Aug. 5, 2020.

Clifton, Denise and Mark Follman. "The Very Strange Case of Two Russian Gun Lovers, the NRA, and Donald Trump." Motherjones.com, Sept. 13, 2018, https://www.motherjones.com/politics/2018/03/trump-russia-nra-connection-maria-butina-alexander-torshin-guns/. Accessed Aug. 5, 2020.

Dáte, S.V. "Pastor Casts Doubt On White House Claim That Trump Wanted To Pray For Shooting Victims." Huffpost.com, June 4, 2019, https://www.huffpost.com/entry/trump-church-shooting-victims_n_5cf6d8ece4b02b1bef091164. Accessed Aug. 5, 2020.

Dáte, S.V. "Trump Visits Church On Franklin Graham's 'Pray For Donald Trump Day' With Hat Hair, Golf Shoes." Huffpost.com, June 3, 2019, https://www.huffpost.com/entry/trump-golf-church_n_5cf463aae4b0e346ce8032ee. Accessed Aug. 5, 2020.

Eagan, Margery. "Race, not abortion, was the founding issue of the religious right." Bostonglobe.com, Feb. 5, 2018, https://www.bostonglobe.com/opinion/2018/02/05/race -not-abortion-was-founding-issue-religious-

right/A5rnmClvuAU7EaThaNLAnK/story.html.
Accessed Aug. 5, 2020.

Friedman, Dan. "Investigators Are Zeroing in on Top NRA Leaders' Russia Ties – and Challenging the Gun Group's Story." Motherjones.com, Feb. 1, 2019, https://www.motherjones.com/politics/2019/02/nra-russia-investigations-david-keene-pete-brownell/. Accessed Aug. 5, 2020.

Follman, Mark. "Trump Spoke to a Russian Activist About Ending Sanctions – Just Weeks After Launching His Campaign." Motherjones.com, March 9, 2018, https://www.motherjones.com/politics/2018/03/trump-spoke-to-a-russian-activist-about-ending-sanctions-just-weeks-after-launching-his-campaign/. Accessed Aug. 5, 2020.

Follman, Mark. "Why the National Rifle Association Is Under Fire Like Never Before." Motherjones.com, March 27, 2019, https://www.motherjones.com/politics/2019/03/nra-russia-butina-torshin-trump-investigations/. Accessed Aug. 5, 2020.

Graham, Franklin. "Billy Graham's son: God put Trump in office." USAToday.com, May 4, 2018, https://www.usatoday.com/videos/news/nation/2018/05/04/billy-grahams-son-god-put-trump-office/34543485/. Accessed Aug. 5, 2020.

Hakim, Danny. "N.R.A. Seeks Distance From Russia as Investigations Heat Up." Nytimes.com, Jan. 28, 2019, https://www.nytimes.com/2019/01/28/us/nra-russia-maria-butina-investigations.html. Accessed Aug. 5, 2020.

Jenkins, Jack. "Survey: Most white evangelicals blame journalists for fake news." Religionnews.com, June 19, 2019, https://religionnews.com/2019/06/19/survey-most-white-evangelicals-blame-journalists-for-fake-news/. Accessed Aug. 5, 2020.

Miller, Greg. "Trump has concealed details of his face-to-face encounters with Putin from senior officials in administration." Washingtonpost.com, Jan. 13, 2019, https://www.washingtonpost.com/world/national-security/trump-has-concealed-details-of-his-face-to-face-encounters-with-putin-from-senior-officials-in-administration/2019/01/12/65f6686c-1434-11e9-b6ad-9cfd62dbb0a8_story.html. Accessed Aug. 5, 2020.

Relevant Magazine. "Jerry Falwell Jr. Tweeted a Crude Message to David Platt Following Trump Drama." relevantmagazine.com, June 5, 2019, https://relevantmagazine.com/current/jerry-falwell-jr-tweeted-a-crude-message-to-david-platt-following-trump-drama/. Accessed Aug. 5, 2020.

Schwadel, Philip and Gregory A. Smith. "Evangelical approval of Trump remains high, but other religious groups are less supportive." Pewresearch.org, March 18, 2019, https://www.pewresearch.org/fact-tank/2019/03/18/evangelical-approval-of-trump-remains-high-but-other-religious-groups-are-less-supportive/. Accessed Aug. 5, 2020.

8. Lemons to Lemonade

Jacobson, Louis. "Who wins and who loses from the tax bill?" Politifact.org, Dec. 19, 2017, https://www.politifact.com/article/2017/dec/19/who-wins-and-who-loses-tax-bill/. Accessed Aug. 11, 2020.

Joint Committee on Taxation. "Distributional Effects Of The Conference Agreement For H.R.1, The 'Tax Cuts And Jobs Act.'" Jct.gov, Dec. 18, 2017,

https://www.jct.gov/publications.html?func=startdown
&id=5054. Accessed Aug. 11, 2020.

Kamen, Al and Paul Kane. "Did 'nuclear option' boost
  Obama's judicial appointments?"
  Washingtonpost.com, Dec. 17, 2014,
  https://www.washingtonpost.com/blogs/in-the-
  loop/wp/2014/12/17/did-nuclear-option-boost-obamas-
  judicial-appointments/. Accessed Aug. 11, 2020.

Tax Policy Center. "Distributional Analysis of the Conference
  Agreement for the Tax Cuts and Jobs Act."
  TaxpolicyCenter.org, Dec. 18, 2017,
  https://www.taxpolicycenter.org/publications/distributi
  onal-analysis-conference-agreement-tax-cuts-and-jobs-
  act/full. Accessed Aug. 11, 2020.

9. Live by the Idiot, Die by the Idiot

Alberta, Tim. American Carnage: On the Front Lines of the
  Republican Civil War and the Rise of President
  Trump. Kindle edition, HarperCollins, 2019.

Fahrenthold, David A. "Trump boasts about his philanthropy.
  But his giving falls short of his words."
  Washingtonpost.com, Oct. 29, 2016,
  https://www.washingtonpost.com/politics/trump-
  boasts-of-his-philanthropy-but-his-giving-falls-short-
  of-his-words/2016/10/29/b3c03106-9ac7-11e6-a0ed-
  ab0774c1eaa5_story.html. Accessed Aug. 11, 2020.

Oakeshott, Isabel. "Britain's man in the US says Trump is
  'inept': Leaked secret cables from ambassador say the
  President is 'uniquely dysfunctional and his career
  could end in disgrace.'" Dailymail.co.uk, July 7, 2019,
  https://www.dailymail.co.uk/news/article-
  7220335/Britains-man-says-Trump-inept-Cables-

ambassador-say-dysfunctional.html. Accessed Aug. 11, 2020.

Penzenstadler, Nick and Susan Page. "Exclusive: Trump's 3,500 lawsuits unprecedented for a presidential nominee." USAToday.com, Oct. 23, 2017, https://www.usatoday.com/story/news/politics/election s/2016/06/01/donald-trump-lawsuits-legal-battles/84995854/. Accessed Aug. 11, 2020.

Swan, Jonathan and Margaret Talev. "Scoop: Trump suggested nuking hurricanes to stop them from hitting U.S." Axios.com, Aug. 25, 2019, https://www.axios.com/trump-nuclear-bombs-hurricanes-97231f38-2394-4120-a3fa-8c9cf0e3f51c.html. Accessed Aug. 11, 2020.

10. Donald Trump Meets the Coronavirus

Borio, Luciana and Scott Gottlieb. "Act Now to Prevent an American Epidemic." Wsj.com, Jan. 28, 2020, https://www.wsj.com/articles/act-now-to-prevent-an-american-epidemic-11580255335. Accessed Aug. 11, 2020.

Burman, Blake. "Trump thinks Russian bounties story is a hoax." Video.foxbusiness.com, July 1, 2020, https://video.foxbusiness.com/v/6168644849001/#sp=s how-clips. Accessed Aug. 11, 2020.

CNN Transcripts. "CNN/Facebook Global Town Hall." Transcripts.cnn.com, March 12, 2020, http://transcripts.cnn.com/TRANSCRIPTS/2003/12/se. 01.html. Accessed Aug. 11, 2020.

Dáte, S.V. "China Demand For 'Other Unforeseeable Event' Out In Trade Deal Was Possible Red Flag." HuffPost.com, April 16, 2020, https://www.huffpost.com/entry/trump-china-red-flag_n_5e976c52c5b65eae709e736a. Accessed Aug. 11, 2020.

Dáte, S.V. "Trump's Coronavirus Claim Is His Biggest Lie Yet – And It Could Be Working." Huffpost.com, April 1, 2020, https://www.huffpost.com/entry/trump-coronavirus-liggest-lie_n_5e83a394c5b65dd0c5d58895. Accessed Aug. 11, 2020.

Dáte, S.V. "Trump Hopes You Forget How He Praised China And The WHO Before Blaming Them." HuffPost.com, May 20, 2020, https://www.huffpost.com/entry/trump-china-reversal-coronavirus-blame_n_5ec44c7bc5b61e42ad3d8876. Accessed Aug. 11, 2020.

Hogan, Larry. "Fighting alone: I'm a GOP governor. Why didn't Trump help my state with coronavirus testing?" Washingtonpost.com, July 16, 2020, https://www.washingtonpost.com/outlook/2020/07/16/larry-hogan-trump-coronavirus/?arc404=true. Accessed Aug. 11, 2020.

Konyndyk, Jeremy. "It's time for a 'no regrets' approach to coronavirus." Washingtonpost.com, Feb. 4, 2020, https://www.washingtonpost.com/outlook/2020/02/04/its-time-no-regrets-approach-coronavirus/. Accessed Aug. 11, 2020.

Nicholas, Peter. "Donald Trump Walks Back His Past Praise of Hillary Clinton." Wsj.com, July 29, 2015, https://www.wsj.com/articles/donald-trump-says-his-past-politics-were-transactional-1438213199. Accessed Aug. 11, 2020.

Taylor, Marisa. "Exclusive: U.S. slashed CDC staff inside China prior to coronavirus outbreak." Reuters.com, March 25, 2020, https://www.reuters.com/article/us-health-coronavirus-china-cdc-exclusiv/exclusive-u-s-slashed-cdc-staff-inside-china-prior-to-coronavirus-outbreak-idUSKBN21C3N5. Accessed Aug. 11, 2020.

11. Republican Requiem

Clement, Scott and Ted Mellnik. "Young people actually rocked the vote in 2018, new Census Bureau data finds." Washingtonpost.com, April 23, 2019, https://www.washingtonpost.com/politics/2019/04/23/young-people-actually-rocked-vote-new-census-data-find/. Accessed Aug. 11, 2020.

Reilly, Katie. "Read Hillary Clinton's 'Basket of Deplorables' Remarks About Donald Trump Supporters." Time.com, Sept. 10, 2016, https://time.com/4486502/hillary-clinton-basket-of-deplorables-transcript/. Accessed Aug. 11, 2020.

About the Author

Shirish Dáte is a senior White House correspondent at *HuffPost*. He is the author of five novels and two previous political biographies, including one of former Florida Governor Jeb Bush. He has been a journalist for more than three decades, with stints at the Associated Press, the *Palm Beach Post*, *National Journal* and NPR. Between Florida and Washington, D.C., were two years and 15,000 ocean miles aboard a 44-foot cutter with his two sons, as they sailed across the Atlantic, through the Mediterranean and back via the Caribbean and Bahamas.